"Important"

"30 years ago, *Why Johnny Can't Read* changed the way parents thought about reading. Today's *Why Johnny Hates Sports* offers an important look at what is happening on kids' playing fields in America and how we can make it positive."

Sam Wyche
Former NFL Coach and CBS Commentator

"Eye-Opening"

"It is time we take a hard look at how we treat (or mistreat) our children in organized sports. Fred Engh's book is an eye-opening account of what's happening in this country and what we can do to change it."

Michelle McGann
LPGA Professional Golfer

"Practical"

"Having kids go through a phase of their life called little league sports is a fun and exciting time for a family. I also know that sometimes parents and coaches can get out of hand while forgetting these are children. Fred's book not only talks about the impact of parents and coaches who lose perspective, but he gives practical ways we can overcome these problems."

Gary Carter
Former Major League Baseball Player

"Outstanding"

"Fred Engh has written an outstanding book on how we must keep kids' sports in the right perspective."

Tom McMillen
*Former U.S. Congressman, NBA player,
and Chairman of the President's Council on Physical Fitness and Sports*

"Sensible Solutions"

"The overzealous kids' coach, the parent who screams in the stands while embarrassing their child and others has long bothered me about sports for children in America. I've known Fred Engh and his mission to make sports a positive experience for all children. This book is a culmination of Fred's experience and offers sensible solutions to the problems that plague 'little league' sports. This book is long overdue."

Bob Murphy
Senior PGA Tour Player

"Positive"

"Fred Engh has written an outstanding book on his life's dedication to positive healthy and safe sports for kids."

Dick Wilson
Executive Director, American Youth Soccer Organization (AYSO)

"Great"

"I am keenly aware of how coaches too often look at the scoreboard, rather than the kids they're coaching. Fred's book offers some great suggestions on not only how, but why coaches need to keep things in focus."

Jerry Royster
Coach, Montreal Expos, Former Major League Player

"Excellent"

"Without proper education and training for the many volunteers who make our programs work, we who administer sports for children would be doing a disservice. Fred's book offers many excellent suggestions that can only lead to better sports for the youth of America."

Joseph Wilson
Executive Director, National Association of Police Athletic Leagues

WHY JOHNNY HATES SPORTS

FRED ENGH

SQUAREONE
PUBLISHERS

Cover Photograph: Photodisc, Inc.
Cover Design: Doug Brooks
Typesetting: Gary Rosenberg

Square One Publishers
Garden City Park, NY 11040
(516) 535-2010
www.squareonepublishers.com

Library of Congress Cataloging-in-Publication Data

Engh, Fred.
    Why Johnny hates sports / Fred Engh.
        p. cm.
Includes index.
    ISBN 0-7570-0041-X
    1. Sports for children—Moral and ethical aspects—United States. 2.
Sports for children—United States—Management. 3. Sportsmanship. I.
Title.
    GV709.2 .E54 2002
    796′.083′0973—dc21
                            2001057828

Printed in the United States of America

10 9 8 7 6 5 4 3 2

Contents

*This book is dedicated
to the cast who helped create it—
Kathi, David, Eric, John, Darin, Joanna, and Pat,
the best team a father could have;
and to the best coach and partner
one could ask for, my wife,
Michaele.*

Acknowledgments

Trying to give thanks to those who helped make this book possible is a necessary but dangerous task. Necessary, because I wouldn't be writing this book if it weren't for the hundreds of people who have helped me over the years work toward our mission of "Better Sports for Kids—Better Kids for Life." Dangerous, because I'm afraid I'll forget to mention someone very important.

First, there is Barry Golombik, who convinced me of the need for this book and encouraged me to write it.

Then, Frank Burns, the man who, when he had the faith to hire me as high school head football coach, said, "If you never want to make a mistake in life, don't do anything."

And John Davis and Thad Studstill who, from their days at the helm of the National Recreation and Park Association, gave me the confidence to move ahead.

Then, Emmet Rodifer and Ivan Mehosky, who, through their efforts with our United States military families, truly helped launch our national program.

Also, Dick Magill and Tom Tutko, the original presenters on our training video for coaches, who set the "bar" for how important coaches are in a child's life.

And Fred Brooks, Bob Spanjian, and Bob Seagren, representatives of three sporting good companies, MacGregor,

Spanjian Sportswear, and Puma, who made the initial contribution to launch what is today the National Alliance For
Youth Sports.

And especially the best seven friends and executive board
members a person could ever ask for, Bob Bierscheid, Bill
Baggett, Bob Scharbert, Cathy Harris, Rick Robinson, and
Tom Streit, along with the guy who traveled the world with
me to spread our message, Mike Gray. And while I wish I had
space to name all of the greatest staff in the world, I'd be terribly remiss if I didn't mention those who serve on our executive staff: Mike Pfahl, the most patient, loyal, hard-working
person one could imagine; Lisa Licata, our bright and ener-
getic new kid on the block; my son John, who bears with me;
Emmy Martinez, my assistant, who keeps me on course; and
Yolanda Williams, the best financial manager in America.

Plus the thousands of dedicated recreation professionals
across America who have added "one more task" to their
already heavily burdened jobs by implementing our youth
programs in almost 2,000 communities across this country.

And finally, two people who taught me that the skill of
writing takes more than you think: My son Eric, a writer who
teaches at Maui Community College, and most of all, to Greg
Bach, who took what I thought was great writing and turned
it into something of which I can be most proud.

Foreword

Kids. What is more precious or important to all of us? As parents, educators, and coaches, we are all working to find ways to prepare youngsters to live in the twenty-first century. Yet, time and again, we witness children being abused in both blatant and subtle ways by the very people who profess to love and care for them.

Over a decade ago, I met a man who has dedicated his life's work to youngsters. His love of children extended well beyond his own seven. He was committed to making a difference for literally millions of kids across the nation. That man is Fred Engh.

When I met Fred, he was a man with a head full of memories and a heart full of dreams. He understood that good youth sports activities can make a life-altering difference for kids, and he set out to find ways to bring these experiences to the youth of today. Because of that dream, he founded the National Youth Sports Coaches Association (NYSCA) to teach youth coaches successful strategies for working with children in positive ways.

Fred has a story to tell, and it's an important one for all of us to hear. By reading about his life as a person dedicated to kids and sports, and as someone who has worked with countless parents and recreational professionals, we can all learn important lessons in how to have a positive and lasting influence in the lives of our children and our children's children.

If you care about kids, the time you are about to spend reading Fred's words may become some of the most important minutes of your life. They will open your eyes to things you may have done in the past—or may be doing now—that hurt children, rather than help them. Or they may confirm that what you are doing is actually in the best interests of children. Or they may present ideas and strategies for doing the job even better. But you will not go away unaffected; you will be changed—I believe, for the better.

Oh, your intentions may be good, and you may devote a lot of time to kids—you are to be commended for that. However, just putting in time is not nearly enough. You need to learn ways to convert those hours into positive experiences that will help the youth of today grow into the healthy, productive adults of tomorrow.

Fred Engh is leading the way for those who are committed to making a positive difference for our children by providing better sports for kids and better kids through sports. Let us support his vision for the future and follow his example of excellence. Our children deserve nothing less.

—Bob Bierscheid, CLP
Director of Parks and Recreation, Roseville, Minnesota
and Chairman of the Board, National Alliance for Youth Sports

Preface

This book is written as the result of a lifelong interest in organized sports for children.

I'm a firm believer that sports is the greatest tool we have in today's society to help children develop positive character traits and life values. But when the focus shifts from what's best for the young participants to what's best for others, that's where problems begin.

Like many parents, I took an active role in the athletic activities of my children while they were growing up. As the father of seven children, I had the opportunity to coach and watch more games and practices than most parents—and a lot of what I witnessed wasn't very encouraging. Win-at-all-cost coaches, overzealous parents, and unruly spectators all share in the blame for delivering a black eye to the youth sports experiences of many children.

I've looked into the tear-filled eyes of far too many young-sters over the years and have seen the pain, frustration, and anger that result from a negative sports experience. I've seen kids turn their backs on sports because someone said they weren't good enough or because they were scolded for drop-ping a ball, making a mistake, or losing a game.

Through the years I have met thousands of parents,

coaches, and administrators of youth sports who have re-layed appalling stories of physical and emotional abuse. I've incorporated some of these accounts into this book. They are offered simply to demonstrate that children are being mis-treated every day in every sport in every community in every state. It's time to put an end to this madness and begin put-ting the fun back in sports for kids.

I have been preparing for this book for thirty years. After graduating with a degree in physical education from the University of Maryland, I began my career as an elementary "phys-ed" teacher. I eventually moved on to the high school level, where I coached several sports, and later served as ath-letic director. I got my first real glimpse of the many problems plaguing youth sports while serving as youth sports coor-dinator for several thousand youngsters in Wilmington, Delaware. Later, at the Athletic Institute in Chicago, where I worked closely with the leaders of America's top youth sports organizations, I began to understand the harsh realities of youth sports at the national level.

By now, I had seen and heard enough. I knew something had to be done, and I knew it had to begin with me.

THE ADVENTURE BEGINS

Because of my deep-rooted beliefs in the enormous value of sports, I decided to undertake an adventure that would change my life and the lives of literally millions of children and their families: The creation of the National Youth Sports Coaches Association, or NYSCA, a nonprofit group focused on training volunteer coaches.

I was convinced that we could make a difference in the lives of young people if the adults caring for them had the proper training and information at their disposal. After years of hardship and struggling to be heard, I believe the message that all children must have safe, positive, and meaningful sports experiences is finally getting through to people. Since NYSCA's inception, more than 1.3 million volunteer youth coaches have embraced the program, which is available today in 2,200 communities nationwide.

With the realization that volunteer coaches are just one aspect of the youth sports equation and that other areas needed attention as well, the National Alliance for Youth Sports was formed under the guidance of our great board of directors. The Alliance includes NYSCA and a variety of other programs devoted to improving the athletic programs of our nation's youth.

MY HOPES

As president and CEO of the Alliance, I've had many opportunities to speak to youth sports professionals at conferences worldwide. Their input has found its way into this book in various forms. Countless hours spent with the nation's top youth sports psychologists have provided valuable insights and data for many of the topics this book explores. I have also collected information from the leaders of the country's premier organizations that try to meet the needs of children.

Furthermore, I have included the results of some landmark research studies that the Alliance has commissioned itself or obtained from other respected organizations. These studies examine such topics as parental attitudes toward sports, child abuse in sports, and the reasons why children drop out of sports every year. The findings are alarming and indicative of the prevailing problems surrounding today's playing fields.

The goal of this book is to make adults aware of their roles and responsibilities in the youth sports environment. Despite the best of intentions, volunteer coaches and administrators of organized sports who have little or no formal training can and do cause serious emotional and physical harm to children, often without even being aware of it.

However, if they are given the proper training, resources, and education, I believe they can be a positive influence on every child with whom they come in contact. Parents must realize that how they relate to their children when it comes to sports and related issues will significantly influence their youngsters' feelings of self-worth, for better or for worse.

This book opens with a review of those problems common to most communities across the country. Subsequent chapters deal with the roles of parents, coaches, children, and the administration of youth sports. We'll take an in-depth look at the ugly parent that exists within every single one of us. We'll discuss what rights parents have when it comes to their child's sports participation. We'll examine the whole issue of coaching youth sports, who should be on the sidelines and who shouldn't, what qualities comprise a good youth sports coach, the importance of training and certification programs, and how coaches impact a child's physical and emotional development. We'll explore what children at different age ranges want from their experiences in organized sports, what role winning plays, the importance of having fun, why children quit sports, and what changes they suggest for improving sports.

The administration of youth sports is often overlooked, but it is critically important to the well-being of the participants. Are programs conducted in a "professional" atmosphere where "winning" is the top priority in the best interests of children? What about safety, equipment, avoiding unnecessary injuries? How do we best handle the hard-core traditionalists, who resist any changes, and the damaging effects of all-star games? We will answer these questions, and more.

Finally, we will offer a plan of action, one based on a lifetime of experience, one designed to help return youth sports to its proper place as one of the ideal tools to teach children the skills and values that will play a significant part in their everyday lives.

Participation in organized sports can provide children with memorable experiences. As adults, we need to make sure those memories are happy ones.

Introduction

Have you ever looked into the eyes of a child who has been yelled at for simply dropping a ball or missing a tackle? Have you seen his pain? Have you ever watched a child berated by a coach? Have you seen children frozen by the fear of making a mistake and hearing about it from the adults? Have you seen a child reduced to tears by a stinging criticism from a parent or a coach? Have you ever watched as a child begged to quit a sport because the pressure was just too unbearable and playing was no longer any fun? I have seen all of that, and more, and after thirty years of observing sports for children from every angle, I am convinced there is a growing problem in this country, and it must be addressed—now.

It's also important to point out to readers of this book that, throughout my career, I have met hundreds of parents who exemplify model behavior in the treatment of children and demonstrate genuine understanding in how to be a supportive parent.

I've also worked with wonderful league administrators who've volunteered untold hours in organizing sports programs for children, with one thing in mind—making it *fun* for the kids. And having seven children of my own, I can't begin to tell you how comforting it was to know that so many of

1

their coaches truly cared about them and the others entrusted to their care.

Kids. Which kids are we talking about? When talking about youth sports, perhaps one of the most misunderstood areas is the age level we are addressing. I should make clear at the beginning that this book is focused primarily on the child who may enter the world of organized sports as young as age four and play up to perhaps age thirteen, at which time, statistics show, most will have dropped out. It is mainly within these years that children are learning about themselves psychologically, physically, emotionally, and socially. Their personalities are being molded. Their minds are forming lasting impressions as to the importance of sports in their lives. It is at this level that we, as parents, coaches, and administrators, will play the greatest role in making the sports experience positive, healthy, and safe. We can see that the results of our children's experiences during these years are crucial, especially when we consider the positive role sports can play in their overall development.

We hope our kids' experiences will be positive, but I must acknowledge that many organized youth sports programs in America today are not so good. Some have been transformed into combat zones where violent behavior is just another part of the game. Parents argue with coaches, abuse officials, and confront parents from opposing teams—often with bloody results. Violence, brawls, fist-fights, and post-game tirades have become an epidemic in youth sports, and it is spilling over into our everyday society, contributing to an increasing display of gangs, violence, drug abuse, and a lack of respect for property and people.

IT'S GETTING UGLY OUT THERE

Recently, in Salt Lake City, Utah, two women assaulted a mother following a youth baseball championship game, leaving the mother unconscious. In Manitoba, Canada, an assistant coach allegedly jumped over the boards and grabbed the referee during a tournament game for thirteen-year-olds. In Whitewater, Wisconsin, a baseball coach for children ages twelve and thirteen was taken into custody on accusations that he had grabbed an umpire, wrestling him to the ground. In Rockaway, New Jersey, a baseball coach was hit with a $1,000 fine and five days in the sheriff's work program for assaulting a thirteen-year-old player during practice. In Los Angeles, more than thirty adults brawled at the conclusion of an under-fourteen soccer tournament game, leading to the arrest of three parents, including one on suspicion of assault with a deadly weapon. In Hazlet, New Jersey, an umpire and parent were called into police headquarters after exchanging blows at a baseball game among grade schoolers. In Manalapan, New Jersey, police investigated an incident in which a youth baseball coach claimed to have been attacked by a father who was upset because his child had not played in a game. And the list goes on and on.

Sure, there are many adults who do a wonderful job helping youngsters have positive experiences in sports. But the age-old ideal that children's participation in games should be fun, and should contribute to physical development and social skills has been buried amid a plethora of police reports, hospital emergency room visits, and arrest warrants. An ever-increasing number of coaches and parents—the most important role models in a young athlete's life—pay lip service to the importance of sportsmanship, fair play, and fun in youth sports. It's all too clear that their real focus is on winning—whatever the cost—and their actions at games are speaking a lot louder than any empty words.

THE PROBLEMS

Studies show that an alarming 70 percent of the approximately 20 million children who participate in organized out-of-school athletic programs will quit by the age of thirteen because of unpleasant sports experiences. That's 17.5 million unhappy, dispirited children. It's a frightening statistic that

3

paints a rather bleak picture of organized sports in America today. The culprits are the adults who, in their roles as coaches, administrators, and parents, have misguided motives and ideals of what youth sports are all about.

The Win-at-All-Cost Coaches

Win-at-all-cost coaches who are obsessed with winning games and championships plague too many youth sports programs. We have all seen these adults—blinded by visions of first-place trophies, playoffs, and post-season glory—prowling the sidelines, yelling at children, and insulting officials. Even worse, many coaches lose total control and get physical—grabbing, hitting, and throwing things—all horrifying examples of what can happen when the adults take over the child's game.

The Overzealous Parents

Scoreboards, standings, and championships also bring out the very worst in many parents, who undergo an amazing transformation once they arrive at the playing field. They yell at their child, criticize coaches, and degrade officials who make calls against "their" team. These parents are loud, negative, and disruptive, a terrible influence to every child playing the game. The parents' perspective can become easily distorted when it comes to the exciting world of youth sports, and their poorly chosen words and actions can cause irreparable harm to children. They have failed to recognize that many of the things that they do to children in the name of sports can actually be considered child abuse.

The Untrained Administrators

Our sports programs are also overflowing with administrators who have had no training whatsoever in how programs should be conducted for children. For the most part, they've been unable to make informed decisions or implement standards and policies that cater to the needs of the young participants. They are one reason why the ridiculous behaviors we see on our playing fields every day have become an almost-accepted part of the programs.

A study by the Minnesota Amateur Sports Commission reported that 45.3 percent of the children surveyed said adults had called them names, yelled at them, and insulted them while the youngsters played in a sports contest. It also revealed that 21.5 percent had been pressured to play with an injury. Shockingly, 17.5 percent even reported that an adult had hit, kicked, and slapped them while participating in sports. Much of the blame for such conditions must be attached to the youth sports administrators who allegedly set the standards for conduct, fail to recognize when those standards have been breached, and neglect their duty to discipline appropriately those responsible.

SPORTSMANSHIP—A DYING IDEAL

Why are youth sports in such a state of disarray? Why in the so-called name of fun do we continue to do things to children that chase them away from the games they once loved to play?

During the last couple of decades, professional, collegiate, and even high school sports have undergone a remarkable transformation. Sportsmanship and fair play have become virtually nonexistent, while incidents of cheating, taunting, attacking officials, and running up the score have increased drastically. The attitudes, behaviors, and beliefs that surround sports at these levels have trickled down into youth athletics and spread like a deadly virus across its landscape. Has anyone noticed what's happening?

THE FOCUS OF THIS BOOK

This book will examine the cultural phenomena we're experiencing in organized youth sports. No other book exists today that examines in such detail these problems, why they're occurring, and what can be done about them. It is based on more than thirty years of experience as athlete, administrator, coach, and parent.

As you read, it's important to understand that there *are* workable solutions available, ones that *can* be implemented at every level, in every community.

We begin with an overview of sports during the last century and how we've arrived at the way games are played by athletes and watched by fans today. We'll look at the behaviors that dominate professional sports as well as issues such as fair play, ethics, and sportsmanship, and how they influence the manner in which youth sports programs are conducted.

We'll take an in-depth look at parents with children involved in organized sports. We'll discuss their motivations for enrolling their child, examine their roles and responsibilities, explain when they should cheer or "chill out," and offer suggestions on how they can ensure a fun and memorable experience for their child. We'll delve into the whole issue of coaching youth sports and cover the characteristics that all good coaches possess, why they often cross the line from stressing fun to winning, and the vital role they play in each child's life.

Then we will look at the children who play these games. We'll look at what they want from their sports experiences, why they're dropping out of sports in ever-increasing numbers, and what effect pressure and stress from adults have on their physical and emotional development.

We'll confront the issues that have been a part of organized youth sports since their inception. Particularly for those children younger than ten or twelve years old, what role does winning really play? How can we emphasize play rather than competition, especially for those younger children? How can we avoid pitting the early maturer against the late maturer? Why do children get involved in sports to begin with?

The administration of youth sports is often an overlooked

aspect, but these behind-the-scenes adults play a significant role in what types of experiences everyone will have. They control the reins regarding policies, procedures, and rulings, all of which impact on the programs we offer our youngsters.

Finally, we will offer concrete, realistic solutions that have proven to be successful in communities across the country. At this important juncture in youth sports, too many children are being deprived of fun-filled and rewarding experiences. It's time to change because we cannot afford to destroy any more young lives. It's time to put the fun back in sports for kids. For all of us.

CHAPTER ONE

The Sad State of Sports in America

L egendary sportswriter Grantland Rice once wrote, "When the Great Scribe comes to write against your name, he marks not that you won or lost, but how you played the game." Those eloquent words have endured for nearly a century as a monument to the true ideals of sport. But in recent years, they have been replaced by a different ethic. Legendary professional coach Vince Lombardi of the Green Bay Packers said, "Winning isn't everything, it's the only thing." So now the mentality is not "how you played the game," but whether you won or not.

You see, the ideals of sportsmanship, fair play, and simply doing your best have been traded in for the far less noble pursuits of today's ultra-competitive, high-pressure, do-anything-it-takes-to-win world of athletics. Accompanying these dangerous attitudes has been the physical and emotional abuse of children, violence, cheating, and the total disrespect for the opposition. It is these disgraceful behaviors that have polluted the youth sports landscape, poisoned the fun, distorted child development, and left behind a legacy of children with broken hearts, crushed dreams, and shattered psyches.

Sadly, simply doing your best is no longer good enough. The Vince Lombardi philosophy reigns supreme in the sports world. The result? A few years ago a *New York Times* article proclaimed the death of sports, as Robert Lipsyte wrote: "Sports are over because they no longer have any moral resonance."

WHERE HAVE ALL THE ROLE MODELS GONE?

America has plenty of good sports to play, but we don't have nearly enough good sports to play them. Over the last decade, there has been a serious deterioration in the conduct of athletes, both on and off the field. We've certainly moved a long way in the wrong direction since the days of Christy Mathewson, the star pitcher of the New York Giants back in the early 1900s and the unofficial "Father of Sportsmanship."

Mathewson arrived on the professional baseball scene from Bucknell College, and he was soon embraced by the public as a true gentleman of the game. Umpires so strongly believed in his integrity that if they missed a play, they would ask the Giants' pitcher what the call should have been. Umpires throughout the league had full trust that Mathewson would call it like he saw it, even if the call would go against his own team. His teammates and devoted followers of the Giants not only tolerated his behavior but accepted it because it had value in his era.

Let's look at some other role models. Jackie Robinson and Pee Wee Reese, who played for the Brooklyn Dodgers, led their baseball team during a period of intense racial disharmony. Robinson is legendary for his ability to endure racial taunts, derogatory comments, and death threats from opposing players and fans, and still continue to play the game superbly. But people forget his teammate, Reese, who was also a true gentleman. One day when the Dodgers were playing in Chicago, Robinson was being abused unmercifully by the Cubs and their fans. Pee Wee Reese, nicknamed "The Kentucky Colonel," asked for time, trotted over to first base from his shortstop position, placed his arm around Robinson's shoulder, and quietly said a few words of encouragement to him. The crowd was quieted by this display of sportsmanship by the man from Kentucky, and the game continued without incident.

There are other examples. Althea Gibson wore her Wimbledon tennis championship with class. Bob Cousy, of the Boston Celtics, would rather get an assist than a basket and led his team to five championships. Gordie Howe, the legendary Detroit Red Wing star, played into his forties simply because he loved the game. Johnny Unitas, the Baltimore Colts quarterback, was always known as a gentleman, a sportsman, and a champion. Babe Didrickson-Zaharius was an Olympic champion who excelled in three sports in an era when women champions were the exception, but she played sports the way they were meant to be played.

Speaking of the Olympics, let us look for a moment at the Olympic ideal. Pierre de Fredi, Baron de Coubertin, the "Father of the Modern Olympics," described the Games this way: "The important thing in the Olympic Games is not to win but to take part. The important thing in life is not to triumph but to have fought well." There is an echo of Grantland Rice in that ideal, is there not? Also note that he makes the connection between what happens in sport and what happens in life, a connection not always made these days, unfortunately.

The Baron, Mathewson, Reese, Robinson, and Didrickson-Zaharius would certainly be out of place these days where sportsmanship has become an off-the-wall concept. The Simon and Garfunkel verse that wonders where Joe DiMaggio has gone, seems fitting. Where have all the true heroes of sports gone? What has happened to the ideal of sportsmanship?

SPORTSMANSHIP DISTORTED

The seeds of poor sportsmanship were planted early on in professional sports and have flourished ever since. In fact, if you look closely at the history of sports, it's overflowing with legends who have made an indelible imprint on the American consciousness despite a penchant for unsportsmanlike words and actions. Knute Rockne is one of football's most revered coaches, but his infamous line, "Show me a gracious loser and I'll show you a failure," has turned out to be the warped measuring stick for the way games are played today. And guard Jerry Kramer said of Vince Lombardi, "He treats us all the same way—like animals," establishing the true nature of the Lombardi ethic.

During the 1920s and 1930s, Tyrus Raymond "Ty" Cobb, one of the greatest baseball players of all time, prowled the base paths. He was one of the five original inductees to the baseball Hall of Fame, but "The Georgia Peach" may also have been the worst sport to ever play professional baseball. Cobb was well-known for flaunting his ego, taunting his opponents, threatening them with his bat and fists, sharpening his spikes, and intentionally sliding into bases looking to hurt anyone who got in his way. He had a well-deserved reputation as a bigot and a hothead. Were it not for his extraordinary talent, Cobb would have been run out of baseball. He was everything Christy Mathewson was not.

Throughout the century, unsportsmanlike behavior has been a fixture of sports; it's just that it has been camouflaged by different athletes or ignored by the media. Athletes of various eras have always "talked trash," but back then, it was disguised as charisma. A cultural icon like Muhammad Ali entertained the public with his flashy words and engaging personality as much as he did with his left hook. While his habit of taunting and embarrassing opponents in the ring entertained fans, it hardly qualified as the epitome of sportsmanship.

It's apparent that by the time we reached the 1970s, this type of unsportsmanlike behavior was slowly carving out its own niche in nearly every sport except golf, which has remained virtually unblemished throughout history.

Tennis is a perfect example of how professional sports can be led astray. The mid-1970s and 1980s marked the arrival of the "bad boys" of tennis. Ilie Nastase, Jimmy Connors, and John McEnroe ushered in a new era with their court antics of swearing at opponents, yelling at linesmen, and throwing rackets. Amazingly, this type of behavior actually sparked the public's interest in the sport of tennis. These players were viewed as personalities who brought a face-lift to a sport that, prior to this, was seldom covered on the front page of sports sections across the country. Sports fans suddenly flocked to events in the hopes of seeing a profanity-laced tirade against a linesman. A McEnroe temper tantrum became even more appreciated than a backhand winner. The public was entertained by these sorts of behaviors, taking another chunk out of what had been a solid foundation of American sportsmanship.

The past few years alone have provided enough evidence of how sports, the people who play them, and the public that watches them have all changed for the worse. We could spend a lifetime running down the list of professional football and hockey players who would do literally anything to win a game. Even trying to injure an opposing player was never out of the question. In 1965, for example, Juan Marichal turned around in the batter's box and attacked catcher John Roseboro with a bat. It was a reprehensible act that may well have been a warning flare that the behavior of athletes was beginning to take a turn for the worse. Since then, we've watched as basketball player Kermit Washington shattered the face of Rudy Tomjonovich; Ohio State football coach Woody Hayes slugged an opposing player who had intercepted a pass; Mike Tyson bit Evander Holyfield's ear; Latrell Sprewell attacked his coach, P.J. Carlisimo; Michael Westbrook beat up a teammate; and Lawrence Phillips beat up his girlfriend. The list goes on; we need only mention the names of players Albert Belle, Bryan Cox, Charles Barkley, Bobby Knight, and Dennis Rodman to recall unpleasant incidents that hit the headlines. We have seen overseas soccer matches turn into deathtraps for fans; each team in the National Hockey League needs to have at least one "enforcer" to match the other team's bully; and even the national pastime now has "basebrawls."

Good sportsmanship may actually be a contradiction in

terms. It may not have played as significant a role as we'd like to think it did, and it may not have ever been an influential part of sports to begin with. For example, the outrageous actions of Roberto Alomar spitting at umpire John Hirschbeck, and Bill Romanowski spitting in the face of San Francisco wide receiver J.J. Stokes were crude and unacceptable, but they're no more vile than many of the behaviors that have become a fixture in competitive sports through the years. The only difference is that with the proliferation of media today, the actions of Alomar and Romanowski were captured on tape and have been branded into our memory banks as we've been bombarded with replays over and over again.

THE INFLUENCE OF THE MEDIA

These sad distortions of sportsmanship did not happen in a vacuum. A great deal of the blame must be put at the door of the media for popularizing such actions. And we the public must also take some blame because we have not always condemned such behaviors. Let us take a look at the role of the media in this area, especially in recent years.

Before World War II, radio was just beginning to fill the airwaves, and television was still a few years away. Consequently, the men who wrote for newspapers played a very influential role. They were the only link the American public had to its sports heroes and the games they played. Writers revered the athletes they wrote about, and much of the fame and popularity that continues to surround legends such as Babe Ruth or Jesse Owens today endures in large part to the newspapermen who documented their exploits. Athletes were looked up to and admired by the public, and writers of that time contributed to those feelings by extolling their on-field performances. Nevertheless, they largely ignored the private lives of the athletes they covered.

As radio emerged during the 1940s, listening to ballgames on a summer night or football games on a Saturday afternoon became a popular form of entertainment. For example, in her memoir, *Wait 'Til Next Year,* historian Doris Kearns Goodwin recalls walking down the streets of her Rockville Centre hometown, listening to the Dodger game and not missing a pitch because every home was tuned to the game, and every window was open. The names of Red Barber, Curt Gowdy, Vin Scully, Keith Jackson, Mel Allen, and Harry Caray found their way into the national vocabulary. Ronald "Dutch" Reagan got his first paying job as a teletype operator and announcer for a broadcast baseball game.

Later, as television inched its way into America's living rooms, the way sports are played and watched slowly began to change. The fights and arguments that had infiltrated sports were being seen for the first time on television screens across the country, and they raised the public's interest in seeing the unusual. It was different, it was exciting, and it added a new flavor to sports.

Of course, during the days of Mickey Mantle, Bobby Orr, Dick Butkus, and Bill Russell, there were only three television networks. Cable stations, sports highlight shows, and twenty-four-hour sports programming were non-existent. ESPN was nowhere to be found. The radio dial featured the "big band sound," not sports talk shows. If a football player bit someone under a pile or spit in an opposing player's face, there was little chance the incident would even be reported, let alone endlessly replayed and talked about the remainder of the season. The nation was stunned to learn how New York Giant linebacker Sam Huff actually made his living when his story was broadcast, complete with blood, violence, and sound effects. The ratings soared, and television executives took note.

Nowadays, this violent behavior has filtered into the public's mindset, and the visual images flashed in front of them every day have had a desensitizing effect. Violent behavior is all around us. It's ingrained in society; it's just another part of sports. Bloody fights in hockey move us; bench-clearing brawls in basketball excite us; and vicious, bone-rattling hits in football draw our loudest cheers.

Many broadcasters have fallen into the trap of believing that the only worthy performance is the one given by the winning team, whether or not they abided by the rules. For example, broadcasters openly admire the cleverness of a team that is able to confuse an official and send a better free-throw shooter to the line instead of the player who was actually fouled. They praise the players who get away with an illegal push, block, or elbow. They glamorize coaches known for skillfully "working" an official in an effort to get favorable calls. These days, disrespectful behaviors receive a shrug, a smirk, and a wink of the eye. It's all part of the game, they say. And the youngsters take notice.

Certainly, there have been numerous athletes who have been models of sportsmanship throughout history, but the media magnet seems to be attracted to the ego the size of Montana, the nasty action, and the bizarre behavior. Especially in this era driven by ratings, the story has become not about who hit a ninth-inning homer last night, but who purposely hit another player with a pitch to ignite a bench-clearing brawl. Most sports do involve varying degrees of violence, and the media are frequently attracted to the physical conflicts inherent in the games people play. Sports stories and color commentary contain metaphorical language that glorifies and promotes physical contact. The result is that the viewing public has, over time, became enamored with the violence.

"If it bleeds, it leads," says the old television adage. The media are often criticized for leading their telecasts with footage of the latest fight, argument, or scandal. But aren't they providing the public with what it desires? So these broadcasts have become a double-edged sword: The more the public embraces this violent behavior, the more the media reciprocates by showing it. The media moguls argue, "We're just giving America what it craves. If they didn't want it, they wouldn't watch it. But look at the ratings." And they are right.

Today, we live in a world of instant information. Television, radio, newspapers, and the Internet intensely scrutinize games and the athletes who play them. Everything gets reported. Athletes' lives are dissected and laid out at the public's doorstep for careful examination. There is no longer a right to privacy for the athlete in the modern fishbowl.

It's ironic that competition among the media for stories is as fierce as the games they cover. And to insure the ratings or the readership, the stories seem to gravitate toward the most violent, the most salacious, the most outrageous. In that sense, "the good old days" are gone.

IT'S ALL ABOUT IMAGE

What has been the effect of all this on today's athlete? Well, it hasn't been positive, I'll tell you that. Once, an athlete would win without gloating, lose without complaining, and treat opponents and officials with respect. Now, however, it's pretty much everyone for him- or herself. Sports have become a stage for individuals who constantly fight for a piece of the spotlight—and the cash windfalls that accompany the glare of success. The emphasis has shifted to style over substance. Now, it's all about who can talk the most trash, do the most creative end-zone dances, and best humiliate their opponents. For the modern athlete, "Image is everything," as the Andre Agassi advertisement informed us a few years ago. Sadly, the ad is right on target.

Today's athletes have shoved their way into the public's consciousness and hyped their way to fame and riches beyond their wildest dreams. Individualism in sports, which was frowned upon years ago, is now heartily embraced.

It's reached the point where we actually expect players to misbehave, and we go home disappointed if they don't live up to these ridiculous expectations. Technical fouls and unsportsmanlike penalties have become as big a part of games as touchdowns and slam dunks. Players today are recognized for bad behavior, not sportsmanship.

Athletes receive ridiculous amounts of cash for playing games today. We have evolved into a generation that wants everything now. The heroes of today are certainly not the same as the heroes of past generations. The majority of athletes today play games to make money, while in the past they played because they had a genuine love, even passion, for the game. With today's average sports career being only about four years long, there's no time to be a hero anymore. And that may be the saddest commentary of all.

EVEN THE OLYMPICS?

Surely, this malaise has not hit the Olympics. Surely, the de Coubertin ideal is still upheld. I am sorry to say, this is not the case. This winning-is-everything sickness has even infected the Olympic Games, once a sacred celebration of everything good and right about sports. The quadrennial events, which had always been the epitome of the truest form of athletic competition, have suffered irreparable damage in recent years. There are widespread reports of steroids, blood-doping, performance-enhancing drugs, and various other unethical training methods being used worldwide by athletes in an effort to cheat their way to the medal podium. World class athletes like Ben Johnson took steroids, then tried to camouflage the performance-enhancing effects; Jeff Gillooly, a "friend" of Tonya Harding, sought to enhance her chances for Olympic gold by eliminating her closest competitor; the entire East German swim team contingent has had its Olympic medals threatened because of charges of steroid use. Officials of the International Olympic Committee (IOC) have come under fire for accepting "gifts," some say bribes, from potential host Olympic site officials, and some have resigned. Juan Antonio Samaranch, President of the IOC, who has taken his own "gifts," sees nothing inappropriate in the practice and will not step down. I often think how disappointed Baron de Coubertin would be to see how the Games have sunk to such new lows.

The continual breakdowns we are witnessing have filtered all the way down from the Olympics to youth games.

18

They indicate that we have entered a dangerous era. If we do not chart a new course, find again the character and sportsmanship we lost, things will only continue to get worse, and we may lose our youngsters to an even harsher reality.

BASTIONS OF HYPOCRISY

The win-at-any-cost attitude may, perhaps, be understandable at the professional level where athletes are paid for their services, but what about the college level? Surely, here the ideal of the student-athlete prevails! We have terrific role models in the persons of Cal Ripken, Jr., Grant Hill, Emmitt Smith, and Pete Sampras. Let's take a look.

Sprawling college campuses across the country have become a bastion of hypocrisy when it comes to major sports programs. Education used to be revered at these institutions of higher learning, but now it plays second fiddle to the big business of collegiate sports. Ira Berkow in the *New York Times* wrote a while back, "It has been said that a chain is only as strong as its weakest link. With the glorification of sports, it turns out, the edification of students is diminished. And if education becomes our weakest link, and entertainment our strongest, then there is trouble festering."

In fact, trouble has already arrived. Thousands of coaches and athletes are prospering despite their appalling behaviors. Many of the so-called policies that university administrations have enacted have simply been cosmetic in an effort to appease the public. But the truth is that many athletic directors, boosters, and administrators are all guilty, to some degree, of desperately reaching for the prestige, national exposure and, most important, the cash windfalls that successful sports teams can generate.

How does Indiana basketball coach Bobby Knight continually get away with the brutal behaviors he exhibits? Simple, because he wins games, and that carries a lot of weight in today's society, even if players and officials are abused and mistreated in the process. Three national championships and a trophy case stocked with Big Ten titles has given Knight free reign to do as he pleases with no threat of suspension or dismissal from the university. Knight's behavior would never have been tolerated if he put losing teams on the floor, but it's amazing how many people can simply shrug their shoulders and look the other way when a chair is thrown or there's a vicious tirade against an official—as long as the wins keep coming. Where have the ethics and morals in collegiate sports gone? They've been dragged away and buried by the likes of Knight and others who follow in his troubled footsteps.

Our college programs are producing a generation of lawless athletes who've come to believe they can get away with anything—because they often do. Players arrested during the week are still able to showcase their skills in front of thousands on Saturday afternoon because coaches have to have their best players available in order to win games and secure revenue for themselves and their universities. When Lawrence Phillips was at Nebraska, he dragged his girlfriend down three flights of stairs and, despite earning a criminal record for his actions, was allowed by his coach, Tom Osborne, to continue playing. Eventually, he helped his team win a national championship. Phillips is just one example in a sorry string of university athletes whose athletic talents have been tainted by criminal activity.

The sports sections of newspapers and television newscasts are crammed with the latest indiscretions from universities across the country. A lengthy list of colleges have been reprimanded by the National Collegiate Athletic Association (NCAA) for various wrongdoings—ranging from illegal recruiting visits and grade altering, to under-the-table cash payments and sleazy boosters. In college football alone we've seen Southern Methodist receive a much-deserved death sentence in football because people surrounding that program believed that chasing a national championship via illegal means was worth the risk of getting caught. We've seen big-time football programs at Oklahoma and Washington crumble because of unscrupulous behaviors, and these are only a small sampling.

I once listened with alarm to one of these similar reports in which a college coach stated, "The truth of the matter is that it is less of a risk to cheat and win than it is to be honest and lose your job for having a losing season."

In recent years, the NCAA has put the following programs on probation: Arizona State's men's and women's track and field teams; California at Berkeley's men's basketball team; UCLA's softball team; Georgia's football team; Grambling State's football and men's and women's basketball teams; Kansas State's women's basketball team; Maine's men's ice hockey team; New Mexico State's men's basketball team; Texas A&M's football team, and Weber State's men's basketball team, among many others.

Fresno State basketball coach Jerry Tarkanian's troubles with the NCAA have been well documented over the years, too. A trail of questionable behavior has followed "Tark the Shark" since he first assumed the head coaching position at Long Beach State and later migrated to the University of Nevada at Las Vegas (UNLV). Although Tarkanian won a reported $2.5 million lawsuit against the NCAA in which he claimed it had targeted him, suspicion has dogged his coaching career. During Tarkanian's tenure at UNLV, for instance, the school was put on probation for two years in the late 1970s for questionable recruiting practices. The NCAA ordered the school to suspend Tarkanian for two years, but he obtained a court order blocking the action. Tarkanian led UNLV to the 1990 NCAA basketball championship. However, his program was later hit with more NCAA sanctions, which resulted in a ban on postseason play and live TV appearances. Later, when a Nevada newspaper published a photograph of three former UNLV players in a hot tub with a convicted sports fixer, that revelation helped force Tarkanian out the door, and he resigned following the 1991–92 season.

Isn't it interesting that these types of improprieties never appear on the campuses of North Carolina, Penn State, or

Duke, perennial powerhouses. Why? Because the leaders of these programs—Mike Krzyzewski at Duke, Joe Paterno at Penn State, and Lute Olsen at Arizona—are men of impeccable integrity who are truly ambassadors for their sport. They've set high standards for themselves and their programs, and year after year, they help their teams reach their lofty expectations—through legal means.

They not only win championships but even more importantly, they help produce good citizens—and good students. Krzyzewski, a five-time National Coach of the Year, has a 93-percent graduation rate among his players. At Penn State, Paterno, the only college football coach ever to be selected *Sports Illustrated's* Sportsman of the Year, has an 82-percent graduation rate among his players. Those percentages are well above the NCAA average for their respective sports, and indicative that the coaches and the athletic directors pay far more than just lip service to the term "scholar-athlete."

On the other hand, some programs are not yet models for the nation's youth. Illegal recruiting practices have become the trademark of some coaches whose moral vision of what's right has been blurred by the excruciating pressure to stockpile wins and league championships. Gifted players receive special treatment. Winning has become such an obsession that players receive cash handouts from boosters, drive around campus in fancy cars, and have their grades doctored to avoid eligibility problems. Collegiate sports haven't exactly proven to be fertile ground for developing positive values in today's student-athletes, turning that once-revered term into just another contradiction in terms. Instead, collegiate sports have been transformed into a springboard to professional sports.

The major problem with all of this is that the effects seep down to the youngsters we see out on our local fields and in our gymnasiums. Watching and listening, they learn the lessons of the marketplace and act accordingly. It's, "Do as I say, not as I do," but children learn to emulate their adult role models, for better or for worse.

HIGH SCHOOL SPORTSMANSHIP

If our young people are going to learn values such as sports-manship and character, surely they will learn them in our schools, under the guidance of trained, state-certified profes-sionals. I fully agree with Jack Roberts, executive director of the Michigan High School Athletic Association, who wrote the following in a recent edition of the National Federation of State High School Associations' bulletin: "Sportsmanship is the starting point—if not the essence—of good citizenship. It is what we're supposed to teach in educational athletics more than anything else. We are to teach sportsmanship more than fitness, more than skills, more than strategies, more than dis-cipline, more than sacrifice, more than hard work. We are to teach sportsmanship. That is our product."

Unfortunately, it's not a lesson that's being learned in a lot of schools across the country. Let's take a look at some sad instances:

- In South Carolina, an assistant football coach followed the referees into their locker room after a playoff loss and was later arrested following a confrontation with police.

- A girls high school basketball coach in North Carolina was charged with assault after authorities said she grabbed a referee who officiated her team's loss in the state playoffs.

- In New Mexico, a father admitted to sharpening the buck-le on his son's football helmet before a game in which five players on the opposing team were cut, including one player who needed twelve stitches. The father said he did it because the referees in the previous game had failed to penalize players for roughing up his son.

- In Alabama, a referee was punched and pulled to the ground by a mob of fans who surrounded him after their team lost in a high school football playoff game. When the game ended, several hundred fans went on the field and surrounded the officials.

23

- In Los Angeles, a high school football referee was assaulted by a player during a game.

- A boys basketball game in Texas erupted into a brawl in which one player was arrested for disorderly conduct.

- During halftime of a high school football game in Michigan, a flag bearer received a broken nose and required thirteen stitches because of a tussle with cheerleaders from the opposing team.

"The level and intensity of the games have increased in the last five to ten years," said Bruce Howard, a spokesman for the National Federation of State High School Associations. "My sense of things is that's led to more inappropriate behavior. The biggest thing I've noticed is the emphasis on winning. That and what they see on TV now. That's what they have to go by. They emulate that."

High school sports have changed dramatically from just a few years ago. Nowadays, there seems to be so much more at stake. College athletic scholarships are on the line, and that's just another step closer to the lucrative paychecks that await at the professional level. I read about a high school senior and his parents who actually filed suit when their son was not the starting pitcher for a baseball playoff game, which they said would cost him $40,000 in athletic scholarships. Thankfully, the judge ruled in favor of the school. Playing sports is a privilege, not a right.

A few years ago, I hosted a meeting of high school athletic directors when the issue of steroids came up. The consensus of the group was that steroids are used, but there was nothing that could be done about it. These were the same people who were hired to help guide the sports programs for high school kids. They put in perspective for me the serious state of affairs in which we find our high school programs. In fact, they were one reason I decided to write this book. I find such fatalistic attitudes to be dangerous to our youth, and the fact that it was our athletic directors who held them, those uniquely charged with the mission to stamp out steroid abuse, was particularly sad.

THE ROLE OF THE FAN

Years ago, you could go to a professional sports event and enjoy the thrill and excitement of watching your favorite team play in a family atmosphere along with other well-behaved fans. That's no longer the case these days.

Spectators today pay out large sums of money to watch games and see their heroes perform. Consequently, they believe it's their right to be loud, obnoxious, and degrading. Even worse, many exhibit violent behavior that impairs the safety of others. It's hard to imagine that new stadiums being built today have to include "holding cells" for unruly fans and that security cameras must be in place to keep a watchful eye on fans who actually throw batteries, drinks—you name it—at opposing players or fans of the opposing team. There was even one game at the Meadowlands in New Jersey where the unruly fans threw snowballs at the opposition and at the officials.

Fans today embrace athletes who win and put unrealistic expectations on them to continue winning. As soon as a team or individual wins a championship, we ask them about defending it next year. If they played their very best and lost, we still criticize and degrade them for not being able to find a way to win. We turn away from those who lose and label them as failures. One simply has to look at the horrific manner in which Bill Buckner of the Red Sox has been treated. He misplayed one ground ball, something that everyone who has ever played any type of organized baseball has done, and because it was an error in the World Series, suddenly he was branded for life as a good-for-nothing, with all his other significant accomplishments forgotten.

THE TRICKLE-DOWN EFFECT TO YOUTH SPORTS

In this chapter, we have examined the ideals of Baron de Coubertin and Grantland Rice and followed the perversion of these principles into the win-at-all-cost mentality that characterizes most sports these days. That includes the professional athlete, as well as the collegiate, the high school, and even the Olympian. The media have their role in this distortion, and so too do the fans and the public, who support their teams. All of these factors cannot help but affect the most impressionable, the most vulnerable of all—our children.

The post-game handshake—when teams would line up after a game—used to symbolize the essence of sportsmanship. Now, some youth leagues actually prohibit the ritual, because more hands are being clenched in fists rather than clasped in tribute. Just as bad, I've seen many kids spit on their hands before they go through the line so the opposing players get a wet surprise. Our morals and values are corroding, and the phenomenon shows no sign of slowing down.

A while back, my wife and I took our grandchildren to Disney World, and there in line was a boy of about ten. He sported a T-shirt that read, "Play Hard. Injuries Heal. Losing Lasts Forever." What sort of distorted message are his parents sending him? What types of values is he going to carry over into the rest of his life?

Here is another disturbing example. I was visiting at a neighbor's house one evening when his son and a couple of his friends walked in from pee-wee football practice. We started talking with the kids, and I eventually discovered they played on the defensive line. Having been a coach, I started asking them questions about their team, and I was impressed with the solid technical knowledge the coach had apparently instilled in them at such an early age. I commented that they must have a good coach.

"Oh yeah," my friend's son agreed. "He's really smart."

"Yeah," his pal agreed. "He even taught us a special way to tackle so we can win against the Lions."

"A special way to tackle?" I asked, somewhat confused by what the kids were talking about.

"Yeah," they both said, and then described a small inventory of techniques that their coach had shown them, each clearly intended to maximize the potential for injury in the player being tackled.

I rolled my eyes at my friend. When we asked why they would want to purposefully hurt the players on the other team, they informed us that the team they were playing in the upcoming game was really good. They had the best quarterback in the league.

"Coach told us that if we can put the quarterback out of the game, they won't stand a chance against us," one of the kids informed us.

As they said this, there was no hesitation in their voices. They spoke with genuine enthusiasm: If they could just maim the opposing quarterback, they would win the game. Both boys were nine years old.

I had already become thoroughly familiar with the potential for irresponsible behavior from coaches, but this was the first time I had seen just how impressionable a young athlete's mind can be. These were children at a time in their lives when they were looking for role models. They yearned to be shown a code of behavior that they could mimic for the reward of acceptance and approval. And it was extremely unlikely that they would question the authority and wisdom of the adult's instructions. At the age of nine, these children were being indoctrinated into the philosophy that winning at all costs was the only thing that mattered, and that cheating and brutality were not only acceptable forms of behavior, but virtuous acts when they lead to the all-important goal of winning. You could see in their eyes that they had no doubts about the wisdom of their coach's instructions.

It was pretty frightening.

As Baron de Coubertin knew, these behaviors can carry over into everyday life. If it's OK to cheat in sports, it's OK to cheat in life. If injuring the opposing player is the only way I can win, then that's what I'll do. And if that's what it takes to get ahead at school or work, then I'm justified. Every child in whom we instill these attitudes is one more person we're sending out into the world who will contribute to the moral decay of our society. We must not allow that to happen.

CHAPTER TWO

The Evolution of Kids' Sports in the United States

Having seven children has helped develop my sense of parenthood in many ways. Something I learned rather quickly was that when a child reaches about the age of eight, you can pretty much count on his or her social activities taking over your life. There are birthday parties, Boy Scouts/ Girl Scouts, sleepovers, school functions, dance class, and yes, "little league" sports. Somewhere along the line, even youth league—that is, a league for youngsters playing any sport— joined the never-ending responsibilities of child-rearing. The best estimates today say that over 20 million children participate in organized sports ranging from baseball to in-line hockey, and everything in between.

How did the phenomenon of youth sports evolve from playing with a bat, a ball, or a peachbasket to playing in today's structured and controlled leagues? In this chapter, we will take a close look at the birth of Pop Warner Football, Little League baseball, PONY Leagues, AYSO soccer, NIHA in-line skating, and countless other organizations that fill a variety of the athletic needs for youngsters. We'll look at an historic meeting that took place in the mid-1970s, bringing together the leaders of all the major youth sports organizations. We'll explore the purpose of today's youth sports, evaluate how effective they have been, and examine some of the problems that have crept in to many of the programs. Finally, we'll conclude with a look at whether we've kept in stride with the goals and aspirations of the founders of our youth sports programs and assess whether we are acting in the best interests of children.

YOUTH LEAGUE SPORTS: HOW IT ALL BEGAN

Most of us never stop to think how this all started and who started it. We just take it for granted that organized sports have been here forever, but that's not the case. During the early part of the twentieth century, organized sports programs for children were non-existent. World War I, the infamous stock market crash, and the Great Depression that followed occupied all of America's attention. There was little time for family fun, games, or athletic activities in an era in which most people were simply struggling just to survive. But things have certainly changed since then.

Pop Warner Football

It all began back in 1929, when Pop Warner Football first opened the door to organized youth sports. Glenn "Pop" Warner was well-known for the many innovations he brought to college football during his coaching days at the University of Georgia, Cornell, the Carlisle Indian School, the University of Pittsburgh, and Stanford. For example, he developed the concept of numbering players' jerseys, started the three-point stance, introduced shoulder and thigh pads, brought in the single- and double-wing formations, and introduced the screen pass. But "Pop" Warner—he got the nickname while playing football at Cornell because he was older than most of his teammates—may best be remembered for starting the Pop Warner Youth Football League in 1929. For whatever reason, football at the time did not enjoy a universal appeal, especially when compared to baseball. Today, however, it has programs in thirty-six states with more than 225,000 kids participating.

However, it wasn't until a decade later, when the seeds of Little League baseball had been planted, that organized youth sports firmly took root in our culture. It was a significant moment in American history as a field of dreams was created for children. All of a sudden, children had the chance to step up to the plate, both literally and figuratively, and reap the fun and benefits of organized play. Let's see how it started.

Carl Stotz and Little League

The name Carl Stotz probably doesn't mean much to most people today, but he arguably had the biggest influence of anyone in the history of organized youth sports. Stotz is the "Father of Little League Baseball," a program that, during the last fifty years, has transcended all borders, races, languages, and backgrounds to bring boys and girls together on ball-fields worldwide to play both baseball and softball. It is the largest organized sports program in the world, with more than 3 million players on 200,000 teams that play in more than ninety countries scattered across the globe. Little League is more than a household word; it is synonymous with organized youth sports in America, as I mentioned earlier.

When Carl Stotz was growing up in Williamsport, a small town in north central Pennsylvania, organized baseball didn't exist. What did exist was "sandlot" ball, as some of us can fondly recall. However, the older kids in the neighborhood never let Carl play with them; he was just a "little kid." Consequently, his life was empty of one of the greatest pleasures of childhood. Later, while working in a local sandpaper plant in Pennsylvania during his late twenties, he came up with the idea of putting together a program for "little kids," so his two nephews would have an opportunity to do something he could never do when he was growing up. They would play baseball in an organized format. They would play in Little League.

31

Stotz discussed this idea with his friends, Bert and George Bebble, former semi-professional baseball players. The Bebbles enthusiastically embraced the idea, and the three of them went to work organizing what would evolve into a program of historical significance, the first organized baseball program for children.

The first pitch of their organized games was thrown on June 6, 1939, as George Bebble's Lundy Lumber Company beat Stotz's Lycoming Dairy team, 23–8. The following day, the local newspaper, *The Williamsport Sun*, reported the game's results with as much enthusiasm as it covered professional baseball.

Each of the three men managed a team, and Jumbo Pretzel was the fourth in their "league." They played their games at a field in a park in downtown Williamsport. Through trial and error, Stotz had discovered that by placing the bases sixty feet apart instead of the regulation ninety feet used in the Major Leagues, a young third baseman or shortstop fielding grounders could throw out a runner at first base. Remarkably, these fielding dimensions are still used today in Little League programs worldwide.

Stotz and the Bebble brothers never could have predicted the tremendous interest that was to follow their tiny "league." The following season, Richardson Buick joined the league, and Stein Service replaced Jumbo Pretzel. Stotz's attention to detail was truly astounding, considering nobody had ever gone to such great lengths to run an organized program. He banned curveballs because he thought that might not be the best thing for a growing youngster's arm, and he designed rubber-cleated shoes so the children wouldn't be hurt by real metal spikes. He even went so far as to address unruly parents in a rather novel way: Anyone who got too loud was presented with a handwritten card that explained the game was for the boys, and could you please leave them alone so they could play the game.

Just a decade after its 1939 debut, organized Little League baseball had spread into more than a dozen states, with more than 850 teams in nearly 200 leagues. By 1947, so many Little League programs had spread across Pennsylvania that a state tournament was held, and the winning team advanced to play the New Jersey champion. This turned out to be its first national tournament game.

By the time of the Baby Boom following the Second World War, parents around the country were eagerly signing their children up for Little League baseball. And by the 1980s, Little League's influence was being felt not only across the country but internationally, as 2.5 million children were playing on approximately 140,000 teams in 17,000 leagues in forty-five countries.

The Little League program has been enormously successful due in large part to the wide-ranging programs it offers. There seems to be something to meet the needs of everyone. For players ages five and six, there's T-ball, in which the players hit the ball off a stationary tee rather than strike at a pitched ball. For those with physical or mental limitations, there is the Challenger Division, designed to give all children the opportunity to participate in Little League at their own skill level. In 1961, Little League introduced Senior League baseball for players ages thirteen to fifteen, and seven years later, they followed with Big League baseball for ages sixteen to eighteen.

As was typical of most of the century, opportunities for girls dragged far behind their male counterparts. It wasn't until 1974 that Little League softball was unveiled to the public. This program eventually included all age levels: T-ball level for the younger girls, Senior League softball for girls ages thirteen to fifteen, and Big League softball for girls ages sixteen to eighteen.

Following the Little League Path

The emergence of Little League baseball to national prominence blazed a path for other organizations to step forward. Early on in its existence, Little League catered strictly to children ages twelve and under, so once a child entered his teen-age years, opportunities to play organized baseball weren't readily available. Remember, Little League's Senior League baseball for the thirteen-to-fifteen age group wasn't intro-duced until 1961.

Little League had created the demand, and organizations like PONY Baseball and Softball and Babe Ruth Baseball jumped at the chance to supply an outlet. It was during 1951 that PONY arrived on the youth sports scene in Washington, Pennsylvania. The original PONY league featured six teams comprised of thirteen- and fourteen-year-olds. It was created as a transition league for those players who had graduated from youth league baseball. Over the next couple of years, PONY's growth was staggering and indicative of the escalat-ing popularity of organized youth baseball. By the end of 1952, the original 6 teams had ballooned to 505 teams that played in more than 100 leagues across the country. A nation-al tournament was put together in 1952, and the first PONY League World Series became a reality.

Originally, PONY was the acronym for "Protect Our Neighborhood Youth." It was the boys at the YMCA in Wash-ington, Pennsylvania who suggested that slogan, but later, a change was made to "*Nation's* Youth," after the original PONY League became an international program.

The organization was spearheaded by Lewis Hays, who was the sports editor of *The Reporter,* a newspaper in Washington, Pennsylvania. In 1954, Hays was granted a leave of absence from his journalistic responsibilities to take the reins of leadership of the PONY league on a full-time basis. For the next thirty years, Hays was always involved in one way or another, acting as the chief administrator, commis-sioner, or president. He directed the PONY program from its infancy as a six-team league with a handful of players to the modern version with more than 400,000 participants in 1,500 communities throughout the United States and around the world.

PONY had company back in 1951. The Babe Ruth League

also made its debut that year. It got its start in a suburb of Trenton, New Jersey, with a ten-team league for children ages thirteen to fifteen, playing on a standard diamond. In 1952, Babe Ruth held its first world series, which brought together eight winners of regional tournaments across the country. In 1966, it created a division for ages sixteen to eighteen and held its first world series for this group two years later. Throughout the early 1980s, it added various other divisions, including in 1984, a softball division for girls. The Babe Ruth League, named for the baseball immortal, currently boasts more than 850,000 players who play on approximately 43,000 teams in more than 6,300 leagues.

The Soccer Boom

Soccer has always been the most popular and widely played sport throughout the world, but it never caught on in this country to quite the same extent. The World Cup is embraced overseas but draws little fan interest from Americans, who aren't likely to lose their enthusiasm for the more popular sports like football, baseball, and basketball.

Part of the lure of soccer—which the rest of the world calls "football," by the way—can be traced to the fact that it has provided a nice alternative to those children who want to participate in a fall sport other than football, or whose parents don't want their child enrolled in a youth football program for safety reasons. Consequently, organizations like the American Youth Soccer Organization (AYSO) have filled a much-needed void.

AYSO was born in Torrance, California, in 1964, following a meeting of local youth soccer enthusiasts who had come together at the invitation of Duncan Duff, a Soccer Football Association representative, and Bill Hughes, of the Los Angeles Scots Athletic Club. Their youth program, part of the Southern California Soccer Football Association, had gone downhill badly, so they thought it was time to breathe some new life into youth soccer. The five participants agreed that the only way to meet their goals was to begin a youth program that targeted American boys.

By the time the meeting had drawn to a close, plans had been formulated for AYSO; Hughes and Hans Stierle were recognized as co-founders. Before the group adjourned, however, Bill Hughes made one point perfectly clear: Each child had to play in at least part of each contest, or the concept would be ruined.

It was Hughes who revolutionized youth sports with the "Everyone Plays" and "Balanced Teams" philosophies that have become the AYSO trademark today:

1. The "Everyone Plays" principle guarantees that every child who registers is required to play in at least half of every game.

2. The "Balanced Teams" concept has two requirements: First, that individual teams be balanced and assembled on the basis of player skills. Second, that teams be reorganized at the beginning of every year. Together, these insure that teams cannot stockpile the best players but must start anew with a draft each year.

In 1971, the first AYSO girls program was introduced, and by the mid-1990s, the entire organization had grown to nearly 40,000 teams with 570,000 children in more than 860 regional programs in 46 states. In 1995, the popularity of youth soccer outside the confines of the United States continued to expand, as almost 300 children participated in the AYSO program that was established in Moscow, Russia.

Today, AYSO is just one of a multitude of soccer organizations that exist across the country. United States Youth Soccer debuted in 1974 and has seen its registration balloon to over 3 million participants, ranging from five to nineteen in age, who play in approximately 6,000 leagues. The organization has more than 600,000 volunteers and administrators, and over 300,000 coaches.

United States Youth Soccer serves as the Youth Division of the United States Soccer Federation, the governing body for soccer in the United States. It is also one of about 200 members of the Federation Internationale de Football Association (FIFA), the governing body for soccer. FIFA represents the global fraternity of soccer organizations that was founded in 1904 when delegates from the national soccer associations of Belgium, Denmark, France, the Netherlands, Spain, Sweden, and Switzerland met in Paris. FIFA's first World Youth Tournament was conducted in 1977 for players under twenty, and in 1985, it staged an under-sixteen world event.

While soccer continues to be a popular sport for the younger generation, as children enter their teen-age years, their involvement tends to revert back to those sports that are more glamorized or receive more attention in the media. Even AYSO reports that 49 percent of its participants are between the ages of six and nine, while only 7 percent represent the fourteen-to-seventeen age group.

Part of the attractiveness of soccer for parents, besides the safety factor, is that it's an ideal way to introduce a child to sports, mainly because there is not much pressure attached to playing. In baseball, on the other hand, there's a degree of accountability built in, since each player has a turn at bat. In basketball, with just five players on the floor at a given time, there's added pressure to perform. However, in youth soccer, it's just kids running up and down the field chasing a ball. If a child goes to kick the ball and misses, it's certainly not as meaningful to parents as missing a tackle in football or striking out in baseball, for example.

In-Line Hockey Takes Off

In-line hockey is another sport that has captured the attention of children. It's become a popular sport in many communities, having outgrown the fad stage. It has become particularly attractive for parks and recreation departments because the game can be modified to fit just about any location. All that's needed is a vacant parking lot or a flat stretch of concrete. In its rules, it resembles ice hockey without the costs associated with renting time at ice rinks or purchasing all the traditional ice hockey equipment.

The National In-Line Hockey Association (NIHA) made its debut in 1993 under the direction of Joseph Mireault, a native of Alberta, Canada. The NIHA was the first association to take amateur in-line hockey, standardize the rules and regulations, and assist in the management and organization of leagues across the country. Until the NIHA's arrival, there existed only the World Roller Hockey League and the Roller Hockey International, both of which overlooked the sport on a global level. Today, there are new organizations, such as the World Hockey Alliance, that focus on recreation rather than just competition. With the enormous growth in-line hockey has made as a sport, one can only assume its popularity will continue well into the twenty-first century.

We Have Come a Long Way

I could go on and on about other organized sports for children, such as ice hockey, bowling, tennis, and more, but the important thing to realize is that sports for children have come a long way since the 1920s. They have evolved into something "modern," and their roots in the sandlots of Williamsport, Pennsylvania, or on the concrete courts of Alberta, Canada, for example, are not always recognized or appreciated.

However, looking back at our origins reminds us of the founders' initial intent: Youth sports were for fun, relaxation, and recreation. On occasion, we need to recall the philosophy of Bill Hughes—"Everyone plays"—and the words of Baron de Coubertin: "The important thing . . . is not to win but to take part."

I suppose there will always be organized youth sports in America as long as there are youngsters to play them and parents to help. I just hope they remember how it all started and the values that drove the youth sports pioneers.

AN HISTORIC MEETING

In 1975, I was hired by The Athletic Institute, a promotional arm of the sporting goods industry, to be its director of youth sports programming. During my initial contacts with these various organizations, I noticed that they all pretty much existed out there on their own, all "doing their own thing." I recall a good friend of mine, Hal Trumbul, who at the time was the executive director of the Amateur Hockey Association, saying he thought it would be great if he could meet with the leaders of other sports so they could share problems and learn solutions from one other. It was that conversation that sparked me to meet with my boss and seek permission to pursue a conference that would bring the leaders of all these groups together. He gave me a green light, but he also predicted that it would "never happen" because all those organizations were in competition for the same children.

I took great pleasure in proving him wrong. I sent questionnaires to the heads of thirty-four national organizations asking if they felt a conference was necessary and if they would attend at their own expense if one were organized. Within three weeks, thirty had indicated their desire to attend.

We convened at the O'Hare Inn in Chicago, and history was made. This three-day meeting, in late November of 1975, marked the first time that directors and key leaders of national youth sports organizations had ever met together in the interest of youth sports throughout the nation. Kyle Rote, Jr., noted as one of the premier athletes of his time and a soccer star for the Dallas Tornadoes, was the keynote speaker. Organizations that were represented included Little League Baseball, the Special Olympics, Pop Warner Junior League Football, the National Junior Tennis League, United States Field Hockey Association, United States Wrestling Federation, Boys and Girls International Floor Hockey, Babe Ruth Baseball, Biddy Basketball, and the American Legion, among others.

We discussed the forty-seven topic areas that they specified. This told me that not only was there a tremendous need for a meeting like this but—more importantly—that the participants wanted to work cooperatively to provide what is best for children. There seemed to be three overriding concerns expressed by the directors:

1. The programs lacked responsible leadership,

2. The parents, regardless of their children's individual needs and preferences, often placed their children in these programs for their own vicarious purposes, and

3. Negative sports experiences could affect children's lives, both physically and psychologically.

It was through these three days of intensive meetings that I first realized something was terribly wrong with youth sports. Here were all these people—heads of youth sports programs—talking about win-at-all-cost coaches, parents who lost perspective, volunteer administrators who had few skills or little training, the lack of sportsmanship, and more. It was a seemingly endless list of problems that had infiltrated youth sports and constituted a negative influence on many of the young participants.

It was around this time that a lightbulb went off in my head. I wondered who was going to take a leadership role and do something about all this. As it turned out, the initial leadership role became mine.

As a result of this meeting, and because of the obvious need to communicate and work together, my first step was to form the National Council of Youth Sports Directors (NCYSD). This umbrella organization provided an opportunity to create the agenda and cooperative arrangements for this group annually over the next five years.

So because of this historic meeting, we had finally begun to attack a variety of problems on a cooperative basis, from a national perspective.

JUST LIKE PROFESSIONALS?

When we look at how we started so many years ago, at the original philosophies and ideals, and compare them with youth athletics programs today, we can see enormous growth as well as fundamental change. While the youth sports system currently in place can and does function well in many communities across the country, the emphasis isn't always where it should be. After all, what are we trying to accomplish with our programs? It seems pretty clear that these programs are being modeled after what we see in professional sports, a concept totally alien to Carl Stotz, Bill Hughes, or Pop Warner.

Just look at how a youth sports league season typically begins. A draft is held where the coaches try to choose those whom they believe to be the best players for their teams, just like the professionals. Later, the best players on each team are selected for the all-star teams, just like the professionals. Then, there are the playoffs, just like the professionals, and the championship series, just like the professionals. In effect, we are treating our children—at least some of our children—as smaller versions of the adult professionals.

The Effects of the All-Star Concept

I have been asked a number of times in my career to attend the opening ceremonies of a variety of programs getting their season under way. What great events! Hundreds of kids are lined up on the field with their colorful team uniforms proudly displayed. Their coaches, mostly parents of the kids, beam with pride, and the stands are filled with happy parents. They're happy because they see their son's or daughter's social life extended into what they envision as a wonderful and healthy experience. The league administrators stand at the microphone and announce the great philosophy and mission of the program. It's what America is all about. It's motherhood, apple pie, and the Fourth of July all wrapped into one.

It all sounds just great, and I suppose it is. However, I have also been invited to many season-ending affairs where, far from the exciting group of hundreds of kids, coaches, and parents, there are relatively few attendees. These are the league champions who receive trophies, awards, and praise upon praise for being the winners. While there is certainly a place for the "winners," we should also honor all those others who were not on the winning team. Are they considered "losers"?

Somehow, we should be able to recognize a wide range of children with varying skills, talents, motivations, and expectations who play the game just for fun. I knew one coach who presented each of his players with a ball at the end of the season, and on the ball, he wrote that player's important contribution to the team. Every kid on his team was a "winner"— and they all had fun. That coach acted in the true tradition of sportsmanship.

In 1993, our National Alliance for Youth Sports conducted a nationwide survey of volunteer youth coaches regarding all-stars. The poll generated an avalanche of responses, indicative of what a hotly-debated topic it is. When asked their overall impression of the all-star concept, 59 percent rated it as "fair" to "terrible." Are you surprised?

Think about it. The major problem with the idea of all-stars is that it can send mixed signals to our youngsters. The regular season is supposed to be a fun time, and a lot of league directors will acknowledge that the primary reason kids participate is to have fun. Competition is stressed, but so are sportsmanship and teamwork. But, as many recreation specialists have complained, once the all-stars arrive, the focus suddenly shifts. Now it's all about winning.

Home Sweet Home

Another example of what happens when we treat children like serious athletes occurs in some of the T-Ball leagues that have been set up around the country to get children started in baseball. Because children have a way of being children even when we pretend they aren't, the result of adults' trying to get five- and six-year-olds to act like serious, competitive athletes can sometimes be pretty humorous.

I'll never forget the very first T-Ball game I ever attended. One team seemed to consist of children who could barely manage to hit the ball, and the other team seemed to consist of children who barely managed to field properly.

One youngster came up to bat and hit the ball straight toward the third baseman. It was about to roll right between his legs when he closed his eyes and put his open glove down toward the dirt. The ball went right into his glove, so he scooped it up, and threw with all his might in the general direction of first base.

The ball arched high into the air and, miraculously, headed toward the first base area. Without having developed tracking skills, the first baseman couldn't figure out where the ball was in the air. Then the ball came down, landing square on the top of his head. Luckily, the league was using a special injury-proof ball with a soft texture, and he wasn't hurt. He just scrambled around searching for the ball.

Later, in the same inning, another ball was hit to third base, and because there was a runner on first, the coach yelled, "Throw it to second."

Once again, the kid playing third threw the ball with all his might, this time in the general direction of second base. The ball ended up against the fence between the right fielder and first base, sending the runner to second base, where he stopped.

"Keep going," his coach yelled to him, so he ran to third base and then stopped again.

No one on the other team had yet retrieved the ball, so his coach yelled, "Go home, go home" to his runner at third. The lad looked confused and just stood where he was. Now other parents from the bleachers joined in with the coach, everybody yelling, "Go home."

So with a quizzical look on his face, he started trotting across the field toward his dugout.

"What are you doing?" the coach yelled in astonishment.

43

The kid picked up his glove from the dugout, saying, "You said to go home."

These were the only exciting moments in a game that lasted over two hours. With the score 36 to 2, they stopped it at the end of the third inning.

While it's easy to see the humor in these situations, there is a darker side that adults often tend to overlook. While we imagine that we are preparing our children for a lifetime of success in athletics, we are really instilling in them at an impressionable age the idea that sports aren't much fun at all. Unless the child has the proper skills and abilities, playing sports can be a difficult and aggravating experience. For many, it becomes a chore they put up with in order to please their parents. When they get old enough to make decisions for themselves, a lot of them will quit sports for good.

The best evidence shows there truly is a need for drastic improvements in our programs. The proof is that more than 2,000 recreation agencies have met that need in their local communities by creating Alliance chapters to help implement sensible programs for the betterment of their youngsters and their sports activities.

WE NEED TO RETURN TO OUR IDEALS

The founders of organized youth sports truly did a remarkable job in the creation and development of their respective programs. They probably would be impressed by the enormous size and far-reaching scope of their creations. But one has to wonder what they would think of how their sports are being conducted today, and of how some programs have drastically strayed from their original philosophies.

For example, as early as the mid-1950s, Carl Stotz was beginning to grow disenchanted with what Little League baseball was becoming; so much of the focus had shifted from having fun to winning games and tournaments, and to gaining national exposure at the Little League World Series.

"It's just a show window," Stotz is quoted in a 1989 *Sports*

Illustrated article in reference to the Little League World Series. "The real value of [Little League baseball] is in the neighborhood league. The World Series is unnecessary pomp and circumstance. It leaves fewer games within the local league because teams have to begin tournament play so early."

When Stotz created the organization, he did so with the goal of giving children a chance to play in an organized fashion with colorful uniforms, quality equipment, and qualified, caring coaches who could pass along skills and knowledge. While that certainly remains the case in many communities, there is also now an added emphasis on winning games, advancing in tournaments, and gaining a berth in the Little League World Series. It's playing in a professional atmosphere with a fancy stadium in Williamsport, hot dog vendors in the stands, game programs, hordes of reporters, and a championship game that's telecast on national television.

How reckless can these championships get? In 1992, they reached an all-time low. That's when the team from the Philippines defeated the team from Long Beach, California, 15 to 4 for the Little League World Series Championship. It was later discovered that the Philippine team officials had forged birth certificates, school records, and other documents to hide the fact that five of the fourteen players were actually older than the regulation twelve years of age. In an attempt to win, they had cheated. To its shame, the team was subsequently stripped of its title. The Committee on Youth and Sports said in its report, "Let this unfortunate incident . . . serve as a lesson to all, particularly to our sports officials and leaders. Let this be a reminder that deceit, dishonesty, and misrepresentation shall never justify any victory."

As I said earlier, Stotz was a visionary. He knew the grim realities of too much pressure and stress on children; he knew how things can turn ugly when there's an overemphasis on winning. Yet, somehow, we have let it happen on our watch.

I've traveled throughout the country speaking with parents, coaches, administrators, and educators, and I've seen firsthand the problems that have a stranglehold on many of today's youth sports programs. I've been in the center of the action for more than three decades and have watched how these problems have gradually gotten worse and worse. As organizations and programs have grown, so have the problems. Things aren't improving, and if we don't do something now, our mismanagement will continue to haunt children for years to come.

I believe we still need to understand these problems and our roles in context, in greater detail. Therefore, in the following three chapters, I will dig into the problems centering on parents, coaches, and administrators. Then I will examine what effects their actions and behaviors have on the children who play the games. Finally, I will recommend a variety of solutions to these dilemmas, suggesting ideas that are concrete, realistic, and practical; ideas that Alliance communities have already proven will work; ideas that will restore respect for and fun in the games we and our children play.

CHAPTER THREE

Parents

A t times, organized sports programs have the amazing ability to bring out the very best in children—and the very worst in parents. Thirty years ago, parents got excited watching their children participate in sports, too, but today that level of excitement is often transformed into abusive and mean-spirited behavior. Behind home plate, the end zone, and the baseline lurk the parents of the "modern" era. There are still many parents who treat the game with respect and promote good sportsmanship, but there are also too many who operate in their dysfunctional world of insults, violence, ill manners, and downright obnoxious behavior where winning is all that really matters. These are the parents yelling at their children, barking instructions at teammates, criticizing coaches, arguing with parents of the opposition, and insulting officials who make a call against their child's team. These are the parents who behave as if they're watching the Final Four, World Series, and Super Bowl all rolled up into one.

It's ironic that nobody yells at a child who forgets some lines during a play, who misspells a word during a spelling bee, or who hits the wrong key during a piano recital. But when it comes to sports, if a youngster drops a ball, misses a tackle, or allows the opposing team to score, look out, because that child will hear about it from the parents!

The unruly behaviors of parents have had a truly disheartening effect on youth sports. The innocence that once existed on playing fields has been swept away as children today are forced to play in volatile environments where games are just as likely to end in fights as handshakes. The pleasure of simply playing has long since vanished, and the parents must shoulder a large share of the blame.

In this chapter, we're going to take a look at those unsportsmanlike behaviors that have become commonplace in youth programs today. We'll explore what motivates parents to act in all sorts of immature ways, and uncover what effect these disturbing behaviors are having on the youngsters. We'll look at examples of what parents do and how they affect children. We'll explore the high profile case of former NFL quarterback Todd Marinovich and how his parents may have contributed to his athletic demise; and we'll go to the opposite end of the spectrum for a glimpse of tennis stars Venus and Serena Williams, and see what role their father played in their rise to world-class status. We will see that parents have a strong influence on youth sports, for better or for worse.

THE UGLY PARENT IN ALL OF US

We've all witnessed parents screaming what they think are words of encouragement when all it does is embarrass and demean the child. They order the youngster to get a hit and demand that he catch the ball; they belittle him when he makes a mistake; and they tell him to "shake it off" when he is injured. Human behavior is a difficult topic to discuss, and when it comes to organized youth sports, it becomes even trickier to understand. But through my years of experience in the field of children's sports, I've discovered that greed, fear, and ego are the three primary factors that influence parental attitudes about and behaviors toward children and youth sports.

Show Me the Money!

There's a lot of money to be made in sports these days, and

parents are well aware of the cash windfalls that an athletically gifted child can generate. But when visions of athletic stardom become the focal point of the parents' thinking, with the ultimate goal translating into college scholarships, multimillion dollar contracts, hefty signing bonuses, and shoe endorsements, the results are typically disastrous.

Many parents are so delusional about the abilities of their offspring they think that if the coach isn't playing their child enough, he is being robbed of his chance of securing a scholarship to a prestigious university. They see their youngster with the good arm or the great hands as their personal lottery ticket to fame and fortune. There was a father in New Jersey who threatened to sue his son's coach because they were using a non-regulation baseball designed to reduce injuries among children. He said the use of this type of ball would diminish his son's professional future. His son was six years old.

Tennis is a perfect example of how parents are blinded by greed. The sport has produced a lengthy list of young athletes who have burned out under the glare of the professional spotlight because of parents who dragged them away from the junior circuit and shoved them into the harsh world of professional tennis.

Richard Williams, the father of tennis stars Venus and Serena, began planning their careers before they were even born. He had learned the game after watching a women's event on television for which the winner's check was more than double what he made annually, running a cleaning business. He felt that if someone could go out there and play tennis for about four days and make that type of money, while he was only earning about $50,000 a year, he was in the wrong business.

That's when he began talking to psychiatrists and psychologists about the tennis life he was planning for his yet-to-be conceived children. After they were born, he began their training as soon as possible. He introduced Venus to tennis when she was four years old and that same week, declared her a future star. Before his daughters had even reached their tenth birthday, he was already inquiring about racket deals for them. During junior tournaments, he would go so far as to tell his daughters' opponents to cheat on line calls, and he'd ask fans to boo his daughters, techniques he believed would "toughen them up." Equally shocking, there are actually junior tennis coaches who have touted Williams as a genius for orchestrating this master plan.

I often wonder how many children are being scarred for life by parents eyeing big payoffs. Even scarier, how many parents out there will try to follow in Williams' footsteps, and how many youngsters will be destroyed in the process?

The Fearful Parent

I marvel at how this fear prevails in sports. It's amazing how some parents will awake in the middle of the night to take their child to hockey practice or skating lessons simply because it's the only time the rink is available. Or think of the soccer mom who surrenders all of her free time to shuttle carloads of kids back and forth to practices and games. Why? Sure, they love it, but the motivation of fear for their child's success may certainly be a strong motivation.

I remember when my son John was about to play in his first all-star baseball game. The stands were filled with proud parents, including my wife and me, who had come to see their kids shine on this big night in their athletic lives. You could feel a heightened sense of anxiety and excitement in the air as the kids took the field.

I couldn't help but notice the woman sitting next to me. I had seen her in the stands on several occasions throughout the season, but on this occasion, she appeared to be frozen stiff with an intense look. She appeared absolutely miserable, so I turned to her and asked if she was all right.

"I'll be OK," she said in a shaky voice. "I just don't deal with pressure very well."

It turned out that her son was the starting pitcher for my son's team. "I'm sure he'll do just fine," I said, trying to reassure her.

The Marinovich Saga

There is simply no limit to what some parents will go to when they think their child is destined for greatness. For instance, we have the story of Todd Marinovich, whose dad groomed him to be an NFL quarterback from the day Todd was born. Marinovich, widely referred to as America's first test tube athlete, was bred to be a professional, a superstar.

As Todd grew, his parents carefully monitored his diet, his physical conditioning, and his psychological development with the express intent of molding him into an NFL quarterback who could lead his team to victory. His father, Marv, enlisted the help of more than a dozen doctors, nutritionists, psychologists, trainers, coaches, and computer experts to aid in every aspect of the development of his young son.

Marinovich became an outstanding high school quarterback, coveted by college coaches nationwide. He wound up at the University of Southern California and led the Trojans to a PAC-10 title and a Rose Bowl victory in his freshman year.

However, he then began to self-destruct under the weighty expectations imposed upon him by his family. He was benched his sophomore year and was later arrested for possession of cocaine and marijuana. He gave up his final two years of college eligibility and moved on to the NFL, becoming the 24th selection in the 1991 draft. He had a short-lived career with the Los Angeles Raiders, and the team cut him at the end of the 1993 training camp.

Since then, Marinovich's life has spiraled downward. He watched the 1998 Super Bowl between Green Bay and Denver from California, inside an Orange County

Jail cell, where he was serving a six-month sentence for felony marijuana cultivation.

From day one, Marinovich's parents had programmed him to be a top-notch quarterback when they placed a stuffed football in his crib. But I have to wonder if they ever took the time to ask Todd what he wanted to do with his life. That he turned to drugs is a strong indicator that he was looking to escape the pressures of having to perform up to the high expectations of his parents and others around him.

But she made no response. It was obvious she wasn't going to speak another word, and indeed, she remained practically lifeless throughout the course of the game. It was remarkable, but after her son threw the final pitch of the game, an instant transformation occurred.

She jumped to her feet and began applauding enthusiastically. "Yeah, Billy," she yelled. "Way to go, Billy." With the pressure off she was a completely different person. In fact, you couldn't have found a looser, more cheerful parent anywhere in the stands.

Fear literally consumes some parents. We fear our child's striking out, missing a catch, or allowing the winning goal. We fear our child will be forced to sit on the bench and won't meet our lofty expectations. We're afraid that he won't be an athlete, or that she might not even like sports and want to pursue other interests. We fear that our child will not fit in, and we're desperate to do anything we can to prevent such a fate.

Too often parents are guilty of thinking too far ahead. They worry about how their child isn't going to be chosen for the all-star team if he doesn't start improving soon. Or they wonder if their child will be good enough for the travel team and what her chances will be of starting on the high school varsity team down the road.

I remember a father who had lost his job because he couldn't force himself to go to work on the days his son played in all-star games. He said he feared that if he weren't there, it might cause his son not to play as well. This made me wonder.

Don't I Look Great

There are a number of individuals who go through life with low self-esteem, and becoming a parent typically doesn't ease those feelings. Sometimes, the way people visualize themselves directly affects how they behave when their child does not meet expectations. They take it personally, believing that it's not the child who has failed, but they, themselves. They are the screamers and complainers, and it's their ego that is shattered when their child doesn't measure up to expectations. It is also the parent driven by ego who sits in the stands with his best friend, mortified when it is the friend's child who is in the starting line-up while his own child rides the bench. In today's society, more than ever, the "yuppie" syndrome dominates the attitudes of so many ego-driven parents bent on proving their children to be the very best.

A friend of mine has an eight-year-old son who plays all sports. His dad wouldn't have it any other way because he was a very good athlete himself in high school and college, and from everything I've ever heard him say, his son will be exactly the same. I know the father will be absolutely devastated if his son is not on the first-string varsity team of every sport he plays. Not long ago, his wife was telling me in a bragging manner that even though her husband travels a lot on business, he still stays in close touch. She explained to me that during their son's baseball games, he'll call her on the cell phone and want to know about his every move in the field and at bat. To a certain degree, it is great to see parents showing support for their child and encouraging him through sports. But when the underlying reasons for their encouragement center around satisfying their own egos, that's when their behavior can begin crossing the line.

PARENTAL BEHAVIORS

The majority of today's parents are a supportive and caring group who do a wonderful job with their children. Unfortunately, there's an ever-increasing number who are disrupting youth sports events with their vicious words, fiery tempers, and out-of-control actions. It's these ludicrous behaviors that have emerged as a rapidly growing phenomenon on America's youth playing fields. These are the parents who can take what should be a good experience for youngsters and quickly turn it into a negative experience for not only their child but the others, as well.

After dealing with many situations through the years and listening to the observations of others, I have grouped parents according to the following general behaviors.

It's Me Out There

Too many parents who haven't been able to make a mark on the world themselves are guilty of trying to make that mark through their children. This is the behavior of the vicarious parent, an element which, when it creeps into parental actions, can severely tarnish the parent-child relationship.

Parents struggle to detach their self-image as adults from their children's prowess in the competition. Suddenly, when the children make mistakes or don't fulfill the warped expectations placed on them, the parents take it personally: It's not the children but the adults who have failed. It becomes difficult for the parents to separate the children's performance in sports from their own identities.

Vicarious parents have become a real burden for many youth sports programs. I had never realized this until my seven children progressed through the organized sports ranks, and I began to meet these adults and observe their absurd attitudes regarding youth sports. These are the parents whose view of sports and the role they play in their child's development has become completely distorted. As Carl Jung, the Swiss psychologist, has noted, "The greatest burden a child must bear is the unlived life of its parents."

Paying for a Parent's Failure

I once was explaining to an insurance salesman what our organization was all about and what we were doing to address some of the problems in youth sports concerning the behavior of adults. The more I explained, the more interested he appeared to be. Then all of a sudden, he interrupted me in mid-sentence.

"You know, you're talking about me," he said. "I'm one of those parents that used to lose it when my kids were in sports."

He went on to relate a horrifying story about attending one of his son's swim meets. It was a really close race, and when it came down to the last lap, he was screaming for his son to go faster, go faster, but the lad just missed out on winning the race. After the event, the father admitted that he had actually gone up to the edge of the pool, called his son "the scum of the earth," and accused him of not trying his best.

"I've never been able to explain how I could do that," the father said to me. "How could a parent who really loved his son do such a thing?"

I've heard a lot of these stories as I've traveled across the country speaking to a variety of groups, and I've learned enough from these tales to know what question to toss out next. I asked him what kind of athlete he was when he was growing up. "I was a swimmer in high school, too," the father explained. "But I was nowhere near the athlete my son was. I was pretty much average."

"You mean you didn't try your hardest?" I asked with pretended surprise. I could tell from his facial expression that he got my point. Calling his son "the scum of the earth" was really a projection of his own self. Without seeing it, he had burdened his son with his own need to feel redemption for all his failures from his past. Instead of seeing swimming as a chance for his son to socialize, be part of a team, and challenge himself to bring out his full potential, he saw it as a second chance to become a winner. Living vicariously through his son, he would erase a lot of the regrets he still carried from his own athletic career.

Close to Home

In high school, my sport was wrestling. Later, as a parent, I watched my kids compete; I wanted to support them, after all. However, I felt a whole new level of intensity when one of my sons was out there on the wrestling mat. It was almost as if I were competing again myself. This is when I had to make a concerted effort to rein in my own emotions. Admittedly, this was not always very easy to do. Part of this was the normal parent yearning to see my kids succeed. Another part said that it was ME out there on the mat. I was somehow reliving my youth vicariously through my kids' athletic activities, and I had to walk a tightrope between providing healthy encouragement and applying vicarious pressure.

All clear-thinking, loving parents have struggled with the dilemma: Where does encouraging stop and pushing begin when it comes to their children and sports? It's a question that has perplexed adults for years and has become increasingly difficult in a society today where being average just isn't good enough anymore when it comes to raising children.

"I think the key happens to be that parents, without being aware of it, are really seeing the child as a reflection of their child-rearing habits," says Dr. Thomas Tutko, a psychology professor at San Jose State University and author of several books on sports psychology. "So if little Charlie does well, it shows we're a great family. If little Charlie is a star, that means that we as parents have done a magnificent job.

Whether or not they're aware of it, slowly but surely, they become involved in the performance because it is a reflection on them as individuals."

The Mother Who Could Do No Wrong

It's ironic that the childish behavior at most youth athletic events isn't on the field—it's in the stands. That's where the normal, everyday moms and dads reside. Now most parents don't intentionally set out to be malicious and overbearing. It's just that the hoopla surrounding youth sports can be intoxicating. Once the game begins, these mature, sensible, clear-thinking adults are transformed into out-of-control fanatic parents. Suddenly they become loud, negative, degrading, and disruptive.

An example of this comes from a most unlikely source. I had a friend who was passionate about the quality of sports for kids. He and his wife regularly attended their child's games, and he even invested his time and money into creating a youth sports publication devoted to all the positive things going on at youth activities. Naturally, looking back, it would have been difficult to imagine two parents with a better understanding of what youth sports should be all about in the lives of children. But then one day at a reception, the publisher's wife pulled me aside and related a surprising story.

"I've got to tell you what I did at my son's ballgame," she said. She explained that it was a playoff game, and the winner would advance to the championship while the losing team would go home for the rest of the summer. This was a very important game in the life of her young son, and he had been looking forward to it all week. "Sometimes I get a little excited during the games," she admitted to me. "You know, yelling and screaming like a lot of the other parents do when they really get into the game." Apparently, this time she must have gone overboard because about halfway through the game the umpire came over to the fence and warned her if she made one more remark, she would have to leave.

She said she was mortified that the umpire had picked her out of the stands and reprimanded her because she couldn't understand what she could have done to provoke this action.

"Anyway," she continued, "I told myself not to say another word during the rest of the game. But then a few innings later, my son came up to bat at a crucial juncture with two runners on base." She couldn't restrain herself any longer. "Come on Jimmy, knock it out of the ballpark," she roared.

A couple of pitches later, Jimmy was called out on strikes on a pitch she was *sure* was out of the strike zone. She made sure the umpire knew how she felt, too. Whatever little bit of restraint she used to have was now gone as she rapidly fired derogatory comments at the umpire.

That official calmly walked over to the fence and exploded, "Out of the ballpark!" in a voice loud enough to generate a stunned hush throughout the crowd. He refused to allow the game to continue while she was anywhere in sight.

"It was the most embarrassing moment of my life," she confided. When she tried to explain her actions to her son and later to her husband, she didn't know what to say. She couldn't understand it herself. This was the type of person you would never expect to need a lecture on how to act responsibly at a kid's game. But that emotional tidal wave had swept over her; and the sight of her son making an out in a crucial situation somehow meant *she* had failed. Sadly, what had begun as a loving and caring desire to see her son play well turned into a disastrous situation that caused her son more embarrassment than striking out ever could have done.

In fact, if you sat down and talked to a group of parents before the season began and asked them how they were going to behave at their children's games, an overwhelming majority would assure you that they would be under control, that there would be no chance of *their* having an emotional outburst. If the above story were shared, they would universally agree there was no way they were capable of such behavior. Yet, during a game, something takes over; it's not their children out there—*they* are out there. As Walt Kelly's Pogo said, "We have seen the enemy, and it is us."

The Major League Parent

Parents invest a lot of time, money, and energy in their child's sports experiences and can become overly enthusiastic about wanting to savor as much success and entertainment as they can get. These are the parents who do not see their child play a game, but rather they perceive a miniature professional player out there on the field. For them, the child playing youth league baseball or softball is not a child of, say, eleven, but a miniature version of a major league player, a professional. How does this happen?

The skyrocketing cost of tickets to professional sports events has priced out many families from being able to attend events. Consequently, youth sports become a golden opportunity for many to become immersed in a team. Throughout the course of a season, parents also get to know the other parents and even grow more attached to their kids, which will spark their interest and increase their desire to see the team do well. Games suddenly take on a whole new meaning, as this becomes the team they follow all summer long, just as they would root for a major league team. The focus shifts, and professional standards begin to be applied. The Major League Parent becomes riveted to the action, as every play becomes one of immense importance. Each game the team wins is monumental, and every loss is catastrophic. As the parents focus almost exclusively on winning, they begin to compromise all the positive values that sports might once have fostered.

Parents can create serious conflicts if they push the child to a higher level of competitive success when the child is only interested in having fun while playing. Quite often, the child will begin to show resentment toward the prodding, no matter how gently it's being done. For all the children who were pushed to eventual athletic stardom, like Todd Marinovich in football, or the Williams sisters in tennis, there are millions of anonymous others whose promise fizzled under the strain of their parents' expectations. And let's not forget the countless other children whose experience was such a miserable one that they were turned off by sports for the rest of their lives.

The Status-Conscious Parent

In my life, I know few things that can compare to the joy, frustration, triumph, and disappointment my wife and I have experienced watching our children participate in sports. There's no denying the fact that parents receive a big shot of pride watching their child sink a clutch basket, score a touchdown, or hit a home run. That's our child out there, and when that youngster plays like a champion, we feel like one. As soon as games begin, there's a powerful emotional reaction in seeing our own flesh and blood succeed. It soon takes over in full force, and it can take us on a roller-coaster ride of emotions.

I'll relate a story to illustrate how a parent, disappointed that his child isn't even interested in sports, will go to just about any length to make the child into something he isn't. Why are they willing to go to all this trouble? Quite simply, so they look good in front of their neighbors, friends, and co-workers. It's a status thing. Some need the flashy new car; some need the latest electronic gizmo; some need the athletic child. Let's be honest, most dads would be thrilled if their son turned out to be an outstanding quarterback. But how many would have the same genuine enthusiasm if their child happened to be talented in mathematics and not football?

This incident happened one summer when I organized a week-long wrestling camp for about 150 youngsters ranging from ten to sixteen years old and having at least one year of experience on the mat. On the first day, the group was divided according to age and weight. After warm-ups, one of the coaches assisting me taught a session on the proper technique of a particular wrestling move and then introduced a drill for the wrestlers to practice. I was making the rounds to see how all the groups were doing with the drill when one of the kids grabbed me and told me of a kid who had no experience and just didn't fit in. While this was not a camp for beginners, there was bound to be a wide variety of skill levels. I figured this was simply a case of kids exaggerating, picking on a kid who wasn't quite up to their caliber.

"It sounds like Tommy here could learn a lot from you guys if you gave him a chance," I said. My idea was to show them how, with a little patience, you could help out a wrestling partner who didn't have the same level of experience.

I asked them to get into position to go through a drill on the double leg takedown, one of the basic moves in wrestling. Tommy's partner immediately snapped into the proper position, but Tommy just stood there motionless.

"Don't you want to learn this drill, Tommy?" I asked.

That's when one of the kids in the group said, "Coach Engh, you don't understand; he doesn't know *anything!*"

I turned to Tommy and asked him how much experience he had as a wrestler. He was so embarrassed that he couldn't even speak. He just stood there, fighting back tears. I soon discovered this was his first time ever on a wrestling mat. I took him aside and explained to him that this camp was designed for experienced wrestlers. "Were you thinking of going out for wrestling next year at your school?"

"No," he said. "I don't even think they have a wrestling team."

"You just thought it would be fun to spend a week learning how to wrestle?"

"I don't know. My father signed me up. I guess he wants me to be a wrestler."

Luckily, Tommy was from the Chicago area, only about an hour's drive from where we were holding the camp, so it would be easy enough to contact his parents, explain the situation, and have someone come pick him up. I took him back to the group and explained to them that Tommy was just learning how to wrestle, that he was going to be just watching today. I told the kids to answer any questions he might have, but Tommy didn't ask any questions that day. He just sat quietly away from the mat looking embarrassed and bored.

Later, when I finally reached Tommy's father on the telephone, I explained that the camp had been designed to give advanced instruction to experienced wrestlers. I pointed out the one year minimum experience requirement in the brochure, apologized for the misunderstanding, and offered him a full refund.

"I don't want a refund," the father said. "Just let him do whatever he can. I want him to stick it out for the whole week."

I explained that he wasn't going to be able to participate in most of the exercises because he didn't have the basic skills that these other kids had developed through years of wrestling. I wasn't going to be able to let him participate in the drills because he'd stand a good chance of getting hurt.

"Well, he's used to that," the father told me. "He's been getting beaten up by practically every kid in the neighborhood. He's an embarrassment to my wife and me. Regardless of what you say, I think a week at wrestling camp will toughen him up a little. Can't you teach him anything at all?"

His father was making it perfectly clear that he was ashamed of his son's perceived weakness. It reflected on him and his status in the neighborhood. It was also obvious he wasn't going to pick up his son until the end of the week. I didn't have any choice. I was being forced to make the best of a delicate situation.

When I explained to Tommy that his father wanted him to stick it out for the week and do the best he could, Tommy seemed mortified. For the rest of the camp, I had him participate in the morning warm-up drills and conditioning exercises; in the afternoon, he would watch the other kids go through their one-on-one drills. He had no interest in learning about wrestling, but when I asked him what he liked to do when he was at home, he said he loved to build model cars and airplanes.

Later that evening, I bought a model airplane kit for him at the local store, and his eyes lit up with genuine excitement when I handed it to him. Each afternoon, while the wrestlers worked on their various techniques, Tommy worked on the airplane in my office.

By the final day of the camp, Tommy had nearly completed the plane, but I was confused as to why he didn't want to take it home with him.

"I can't," he said. "My dad doesn't like me to make them. He says it's just for sissies."

I remember thinking how sad it was that this child had to suppress so much of what he thought of as fun. His father had an ideal of what his son should be like, tough and athletic. That was the image, the status, he wanted reflected on himself, his family, and his son. He seemed completely unwilling to accept any other option, and I couldn't help but think that this kid could make one heck of an engineer someday.

Not all children are athletes, but they can still be great kids. And they will still survive in this world. However, for a lot of parents that's a tough pill to swallow, one that many refuse to swallow. When we encourage our children's natural inclinations, they stand a good chance of accepting and overcoming the challenges that will come along in their struggle to reach their full potential as individuals. But when we crush their individual spirit with discouragement and only support them when they conform to our desires for status and recognition, we create a world of alienation and frustration for them. Is that what we really want?

Some Parents Are Kids, Too

Maturity demands that people anticipate the consequences of their actions and take responsibility for them. However, immature parents don't anticipate the consequences of their boorish behavior, but just act impulsively, without thinking. And immature parents don't take responsibility, but blame the referee, the coach, or the mistakes of others, never the real villain.

Parents must understand that their behavior at games has an enormous impact on every single child participating in the event. The children hear the parent who applauds when another child strikes out. They hear the swear words and insults directed at an umpire. They hear the second-guessing and bad-mouthing of their coach. Not only does this immature behavior set a bad example for other children, but it opens the door for them to see such actions as permission to behave in the same cruel ways themselves. Bad behavior breeds bad behavior, and this vicious cycle just keeps churning right along. But the immature parent either doesn't know or doesn't care.

I will never forget my very first video shoot of a soccer game. We were doing the video of kids ages seven and eight playing in a demonstration game to show examples of positive and negative behaviors. I noticed from the moment the first whistle blew to start the game that this one woman constantly followed her son from one end of the field to the other, screaming at him to "hustle." The youngster obviously had little idea what his mom meant, and I kept thinking that all he ever wanted to do was come out and play, not be made a fool of by his mom.

Finally, near the end of the game and exhausted from running all over the field, the youngster, practically in tears, walked off the field. He said, "Mommy, I hate soccer. I'm not playing anymore."

Several of us who observed the incident later wondered what was going to happen to that poor kid. It was evident to me that so many parents really are clueless when it comes to youth sports.

As I said, maturity requires that people anticipate and take responsibility for the consequences of their actions. This mother did not do so. She had no idea that she had ruined the game for her son, nor did she take any responsibility for her actions. Because she did not anticipate the consequences of her behavior, she blamed the coach, the referee, the game itself, or the crowd, when all she had to do to find the real culprit was to look in the mirror.

So it is with immature parents who berate the coach, insult the referee, or scorn the opposition. They don't think of the consequences; they take no responsibility; and kids are the losers. This type of parent appears in many other forms, too. I was literally speechless when I read a newspaper article about a parent in Michigan who actually sued the umpire of one of his child's games because he said the ump's calls had cost his son's team the game. What's next?

Parental Behavior Can Be Destructive

I have tried to place a variety of parental behaviors in general categories, based on their most prominent behavior, but you should understand there may be some overlap. For example, the vicarious parent who competes *through* her child may also be a fanatic who screams at the "incompetent" coach; the immature parent who cannot take responsibility for his actions may also seek to push his child to athletic success so he can "cash in" at the Major League level. The important point to realize, however, is that such parental behaviors are destructive.

THE EFFECTS OF PARENTAL BEHAVIORS

When we behave out of greed, fear, or ego, we parents may be meeting our needs of the moment, but we are also teaching our children lessons they may carry for a lifetime. We must realize that our actions have consequences, and we don't always know what they are.

A Story Heard Too Often

It's very easy for parents to fall into the trap of rewarding their children when they deliver a game-winning hit or produce a game-saving tackle. But children deserve a parent's love and a post-game hug regardless of whether they went 4-for-4 or 0-for-4.

Love based on our children's performance on the field is a lethal formula that many parents unintentionally apply. This is conditional love, and it is a sure-fire way to create all sorts of emotional problems for the youngsters. Children deserve praise and respect for simply doing their best, regardless of what the scoreboard or the stat sheet says when the game is over.

"We drag kids off the field and say to them, 'I cannot believe how you embarrassed me by not hitting the ball. It was a perfect pitch. Your mother and I were counting on you, son, to hit it over the fence. We would have been so proud if you simply could have hit a home run.' But that's not what it's all about," said Mark Kennedy, Alabama Supreme Court Justice, who was the keynote speaker at a child abuse prevention conference the Alliance held a few years ago. "Our children are gifts to us. It will be in their hearts that they remember their parents, and I hope that when my children remember me, they will look back and say, 'Here was a man who loved his children. Here was a man who was always there for me, even though I may have never won, even though I didn't make straight A's, and even though I never made the winning touchdown.'"

I was playing golf with a friend of mine who asked me about an article he'd read in the local newspaper about my organization's efforts to prevent abuse in youth sports. He seemed interested in the subject, and before long, I had started in on one of my impromptu lectures on the misconceptions people have about youth sports:

"One of the big problems is that most parents don't think of the effects of sports much more than they do the effects of sending their kid to a birthday party. But sports can have a major impact on a child's life."

During the remainder of the afternoon, he shared with me the details of the difficult and strained relationship he had

had with his father. He told me that over the years, they had remained cold and distant from each other, and because he had three sisters, it was pretty easy for the father and son to avoid serious interaction at family gatherings. When they did talk, their discussions were brief and never concerned matters central to their hearts.

It seemed as if an invisible wall had mysteriously sprung up between them. When his wife would ask him about his relationship with his father, all he could say was that they "just didn't connect."

The first bricks in that wall had been laid during the son's youth league baseball days. The father had developed a ritual; he would take his son out to eat wherever he wanted after the game—but with one condition. The son had to meet a certain performance standard. If he hit less than .500 for the game or made any errors in the field, there was no reward afterward, just a return trip home. There were a lot of games, my friend told me, when he would play a great game but still not meet the conditions. He recalled one time when he got the game-winning hit, but it had been his only hit of the game.

"I would go out there and play my guts out," he said to me, "but he was never pleased. I never felt like I was good enough to make him proud of me." It was obvious to me that he had never gotten over the feeling that he had let his father down; the feeling that nothing he could do would ever be good enough.

It may not seem that important to an adult, but in the child's mind, he was being taught that doing his best wasn't good enough. To a child who wants to please his parents, such a feeling can be devastating. If doing your best isn't going to win approval, than why bother at all?

After years of struggling to meet his father's high expectations, and failing, he gave up. Rather than deal with feeling like a loser in his father's eyes, he quit playing baseball altogether—and put more bricks in the invisible wall between them.

Only recently, his father confessed that he had sometimes felt guilty about the way he had treated the son, but at the time, he felt he was conditioning his son to set goals, to strive to be the very best. If they could have had a heart-to-heart talk a long time ago, the whole problem might have been straightened out. But when feelings become hurt and resentments start to form, human beings can fall into amazingly stubborn patterns of behavior.

You're Not Good Enough

Dr. Joel Fish, founder and director of the Center for Sports Psychology in Philadelphia, related a shocking story to me at a recent conference. A ten-year-old girl had stopped eating. She explained to Dr. Fish that she had done so because she didn't "deserve" food. She explained that she wasn't performing well in her track meets; her times had not improved as she and her coach had hoped.

Her parents didn't ask if she had done her best. Rather, they expressed their great disappointment in her. As a result, she lost confidence in herself and in her abilities. She began to think of herself as "not good enough," and her race times still showed no improvement. A vicious cycle had started, with no end in sight. This little girl's self-esteem had vanished—and she was only ten. It's scary to consider the emotional baggage this child is going to carry into adulthood simply because she wasn't running as fast as her parents thought she could.

When Pushing Becomes Shoving

I saw a different kind of outcome when friends of my son Patrick used to visit our house to use the backyard pool. During a Saturday in the middle of the summer, the whole gang was playing water polo in the pool. They needed an even number of players to balance out the teams, but Jack refused to join in. Inevitably, the kids started splashing him and teasing him for refusing to join them in the pool. Soon, he went into our house to seek refuge behind the sliding glass doors.

"What's up?" I asked him.

"I'm not allowed to swim."

I could see that he was pretty upset, so out of curiosity, I asked him why he wasn't allowed to go swimming, assuming there must be some medical reason.

It turned out that the night before, he hadn't pitched very well for his baseball team. After he had walked several batters and thrown two wild pitches, his coach had taken him out in the third inning. Later, when his father questioned him about why he had struggled with his control, Jack admitted he had spent several hours that day swimming and playing with his friends in our pool, and Jack allowed that maybe his arm was a little tired. You see, his father had elicited a promise from Jack that he would stay out of our swimming pool for the rest of the baseball season—which would last through most of the hot Florida summer—and now Jack had "broken his word," and it had "cost his team the win."

Jack's father is indicative of the type of parent who only wanted the best for his son but went about it in completely the wrong way. When Jack was big enough to put a glove on his hand, I saw him out in the front yard where his dad was teaching him skills. But I first sensed trouble when he was five years old. He was on the same T-ball team as my son, and his dad would complain that the game wasn't enough like the "real baseball" his kid was ready to play.

With the long hours of practice that Jack put in, he easily outperformed most of the other kids each season, which certainly satisfied his father's zealous dream of raising a champion athlete. As time went on, Jack was encouraged to devote more and more of his free time to baseball. By the time he was seven, he was playing organized baseball in both spring and fall leagues. During the off-season, he followed a regimented practice schedule that his father had devised. His pitching got better and better.

But now he had a secret he wasn't sharing with his father.

When he had told me the story of his promise to stay out of the swimming pool, I mentioned that I was very impressed with his dedication to baseball, giving up the chance to play with his friends.

"You must really love baseball," I said.

"I hate baseball," he snapped. "I never get to have any fun anymore."

"Does your father know how you feel?"

With the mention of his father, Jack quickly clammed up. "My dad just wants me to do good in baseball," and stalked away.

This is the way it is with a lot of youngsters who have pressure on them to be athletically competitive at an early age. It's natural for children to want to please their parents. But when they have to give up needs that are intrinsic to their youthful nature, like playing with friends, and are forced to take on the structure and discipline of competitive athletics long before they're ready for it, the resentment and negative feelings are bound to surface at some point.

Inside of this boy, there was a talented and enthusiastic baseball player waiting to blossom, but his father was simply pushing way too hard, too soon. He just didn't realize the consequences of his actions.

CONCLUSION

Parents want—and deserve—the very best for their child. Whether it's dance recitals or soccer games, they want to see their child succeed. And considering that most parenting is really on-the-job training, most parents do a really decent job. They keep a sense of perspective, set reasonable rules, and care deeply about the welfare of their children. Of course, there are others who have severe problems as parents, and in this chapter, we've examined their behaviors, especially as they affect their children and youth sports.

It's really no big mystery why so many parents lose perspective while watching their children participate. Athletic competition places their children in a vulnerable position, and the natural impulse is to try and control things, to insure that nothing bad happens. This is an extremely difficult position to be in, wanting to control something—the competition—that by its very nature is uncontrollable. However, this is what happens when the impulse of the love toward their children becomes transformed into the types of irrational behaviors discussed in this chapter.

The problems we've covered in this section are widespread, but they certainly don't reflect the behaviors of *all* parents. There are many, many wonderful people who are doing an outstanding job. The problem is that there are also a lot of adults who simply stand by and watch the unsportsmanlike behaviors of others, actions that are totally unacceptable in a youth sports environment, as we have seen.

By doing nothing, these parents indicate that such actions are acceptable. Their silence suggests approval. They forget, "If you are not part of the solution, you are part of the problem." They may believe that discretion is the better part of valor, but in the process, they allow destructive behaviors to spread, unchecked.

What can be done? Later, we'll take a look at how parents can police themselves and others around them to insure that they don't stray into irrational behavior. All hope is not lost. It's certainly not too late to start changing many of the unwanted behaviors that have done such terrible damage in our communities across the country.

CHAPTER FOUR

The Youth Coach

Coaching in an organized youth sports program today really has less to do with the youngsters who actually play the game and more to do with what the scoreboard reads when the game is finished. What were at one time the traditional skills of coaching—teaching, encouraging, and supporting—have disintegrated in an atmosphere that places a greater emphasis on gaining victories at whatever the cost. Nowadays, coaches are defined by how many trophies line their mantel. The higher the winning percentage the better the coach, claims the modern wisdom.

It should come as no great surprise that approximately 85 percent of the volunteer coaches have their own child on the team. After all, having a child participating in sports is the single greatest incentive for an adult to get involved. This parental involvement is vital because without the parents' taking on these coaching roles, organized sports programs would probably not be in existence today. However, their involvement is usually accompanied by a serious lack of knowledge about the sport itself, and about how to deal effectively with both children and parents in a sports setting. These weaknesses often frustrate the coach and hamper the youngsters' growth and development.

In this chapter, we're going to take a look at the importance of the coach, examine problems with coaching, explore the disturbing mentality of win-at-all-cost coaches, examine the attitudes of the macho coaches, and suggest some things that need to be done to support good coaching in our communities.

THE IMPORTANCE OF COACHES

In many respects, the coach on the field operates much like the teacher in the classroom. The certified professional teacher takes over when the child goes to school, and the coach takes over when the child tries out for the team. Except, perhaps, the coach is not properly trained or held accountable for his or her actions. More on that later. Still, the major tasks of the coach involve teaching the basic skills of the game, instructing the youngsters in the rules and the mechanics of the sport, and supporting the team members when they face their inevitable disappointments, trials, and errors. The coach should remember that he or she operates as an extension of the players' parents, and treat the children as if they were his or her own. Coaches, whether they're store owners, sales people, truck drivers, executives, auto mechanics, or farmers, are entrusted with providing children with a healthy, safe, and positive sports experience.

Like parents and teachers, coaches can have an enormous effect on the lives of the children entrusted to their care. Their influence, for better or for worse, can last a lifetime. Let me give you a few ways in which this is true.

The Kids' Greatest Role Models

Coaches, whether they like it or not, are very important role models for America's future, and they don't even know it. Let's explore that idea a bit.

In my radio appearances across the country, I've been asked by listeners how I feel about the poor example that professional athletes have set as role models. My response is that the true role models for children are not the professional athletes they may see on television, but their own local youth coaches. It is here that they will truly learn the lessons of life.

Children, especially those below the age of ten, are extremely impressionable. Therefore, if "Coach" screams and curses at officials, encourages cheating, smokes or chews tobacco, then these become acceptable behaviors in the eyes of the children. The reverse is true also. If "Coach" emphasizes good sportsmanship, genuine courtesy, and good, clean fun, then these become the acceptable behaviors!

I can remember our son John's coach as if it were yesterday. His name was Phil Knight, and I believe to this day that Coach Knight instilled some wonderful traits in my son, as well as the other kids on the team. Coach Knight demanded respect, and with his fair sense of discipline, you could see all players on the team maturing as responsible young men. They would respond to his every command with a "yes, sir" response and listen intently as he planned strategy and taught techniques.

I believe every coach in youth sports is a role model. That's the bottom line. And the fact of the matter is that for many children who come from single-parent homes or whose parents don't take an active and caring role in their lives, the coach is the only role model for the child to imitate.

I read with great interest a Purdue University study that found that 83 percent of the girls and 70 percent of the boys polled indicated their coach was the most important influence in whether they would take part in aggressive acts that broke the rules of the sport they were playing.

A few years ago, the Alliance commissioned a study on anabolic steroids that polled ten- to fourteen-year-olds. One of the questions in the study asked whom they thought should be primarily responsible for teaching them and their teammates about anabolic steroids. Their number one answer was, you guessed it, their coaches.

Perhaps, the best example of a coach's influence occurred

when I discussed coaching at a seminar in Louisiana. Following the session a man about forty-five years old approached me and said that he had a story for me. He told me he had been a coach, and that not long ago, he had received a call from one of his former players whom he had coached about fifteen years before. The player had asked the man if he would be his best man at his wedding. The coach admitted he was surprised and asked the player why he would want him when there were so many of his buddies who could fill that role. The young man went on to say that the coach was the person who had made him what he was today, that without the encouragement and good direction the coach had given him, he wasn't sure where he would have ended up since his dad had left home when he was seven. Most coaches do not realize just how strong an influence they have on their youngsters.

The Coach's Influence

I said before that the job of coach is more than simply teaching skills, organizing practices, and filling out lineup cards, yet there are important aspects to those tasks, too.

I recall a youth league baseball game in which the batter topped the ball down the first base line. When the ball rolled foul, the first baseman slapped it *really* foul, and the umpire correctly yelled, "Foul."

The offensive coach sneered and laughed at the first baseman, saying, "Hey, why did he have to slap the ball so far?"

His players said nothing, but they did roll their eyes. They knew that slapping the foul ball was not only legal, it was smart. They knew that according to the rules, if a foul ball rolls back into fair territory, it will then be a fair ball. So when the fielder slapped the foul ball, he made sure it stayed foul. He and his teammates knew the rule, but their coach did not. More important, he did not command the respect of his players, the first step in the breakdown of discipline.

That coach also did not instill respect for the *game*, another aspect of the coaching responsibility often overlooked.

Sure, he should know the rulebook, teach the rules, and play by the rules, but he should also know the game, love the game, respect the game, teach the tradition of the game. He should know about Bill Hughes and the "everyone plays" philosophy. He should know about teamwork, fun, sportsmanship, honesty, and effort. Kids are not going to get such values from the professionals or from the media; they need to get them from an informed, caring coach.

And that's a problem these days. To find out why, we need to look at exactly who are the coaches, and why they get involved, and with what kind of training.

WHO COACHES AND WHY?

These days, anyone can call himself a coach. All he has to do is go down to the local recreation department and sign up, no questions asked. The likelihood is that he will probably even be welcomed with open arms. In most cases there won't be a screening process. He won't have to demonstrate any knowledge or skills of the sport. He won't have to present any proof that he has received any type of training to coach a group of kids in sports. All he has to do is sign up, and all of a sudden he is the coach of the Tigers or the Bears or the Lions. Now he has the title of "coach" on the back of his shirt and fifteen or so very impressionable youngsters staring up at him.

I've always found it absurd that in our society, we require plumbers and electricians to be certified to work on our house. We require counselors and teachers to be certified to work in our schools. Yet a person who can have such a profound influence on our children doesn't have to have a single minute of training in the do's and do nots of coaching kids.

America's Models for Volunteerism

Now, without question, there are many well-intentioned people who sign up to be coaches. Many, through their knowledge and instincts, are well equipped to do a great job of coaching. However, for the most part, these are often the exceptions to the rule, and the rest of the pack runs the gamut from good people who lack the practical knowledge needed for effective coaching to child molesters looking to prey on easy targets.

Many moms and dads get involved for all the right reasons. They want to spend quality time with their children, and there's really no better place for that to happen than in athletics. It's through their role as coach that they can introduce their offspring to the sport, teach them skills, and strengthen the parent-child bond. In an era of long workdays and hectic schedules, the small number of hours each week devoted to practice and games are quite often the only times a parent and child actually have a chance to participate in an activity together.

However, there are other parents who get involved for reasons that will, on the surface, appear genuine, but are often shrouded with ulterior motives. Perhaps, the parent thinks his child may not get much of an opportunity to play unless he steps forward, becomes the coach, and thereby determines the playing time of each child. Maybe, in the back of a parent's mind, he believes his son or daughter is going to be a talented pitcher, and the only way to insure he or she will actually be a pitcher on the team is to become the coach.

Then there are those parents who "volunteer" to coach who really never wanted to do so in the first place. Nevertheless, I have often wondered if the world of children's sports has not, in fact, recruited more volunteers than in any other area of society, and I believe these good people deserve our deepest gratitude.

Getting Drafted

When you stop to consider there are an estimated 2 million or more volunteer youth coaches, you can't help but wonder how many of them are "drafted" into the position because there simply was no one else willing to step forward and assume the responsibility. It happens all the time. A typical scenario that unfolds in communities all across the country is similar to the following example, which perhaps even you have experienced.

On a Saturday morning, you take your child to the local parks and recreation department to sign up for soccer because your next door neighbor's kid is playing, and your child wants to play, too. As you're signing your child up, the guy on the other side of the table forever alters your life when he says to you, "Now you realize, in order to make this program work, we're going to need people to volunteer to coach. You look like just the kind of guy that will help us out. What do you say we put you down to coach a team? You'll have a great group of kids to work with."

Before you even have time to consider the enormous implications of the request—or turn and sprint to the exit—you're being handed a list of names, addresses, and phone numbers. In just a matter of seconds, you realize that this complete stranger has turned your world upside down and created chaos with your nights and weekends, which will now be booked with practices, games, and tournaments.

You thought having one child was difficult? Now you've got fifteen or so to worry about. And their parents. You had only planned to blend in on the sidelines with all the other parents during games, and perhaps knock off a good book during practices. You never dreamed that you'd be roped into directing a youth soccer team; coaching a sport you never even played growing up; coaching a sport where your knowledge is pretty much limited to one word: GOOOOOOOAAAAL! Then, after looking at the rule book, you realize this is a sport where the rules are as foreign to you as the majority of the professionals who play it.

So before you even know it, Tuesday night arrives, and your child and a bunch of other kids are meeting you at this huge, empty field, and everyone is calling you a name you never dreamed of, asking you an embarrassing question, "Hey, Coach, did anyone bring a ball?"

Millions of moms and dads have gone through this experience, and I'd say that the overwhelming majority of adults who find themselves in this predicament (some may refer to it in less unsavory terms) are caring individuals. After all, the odds are they couldn't have been arm-twisted into coaching in the first place if they didn't have some genuine concern for the kids and their local sports program. But despite the best of intentions, many do a horrific job that can have dramatic consequences, both physically and psychologically, on the children.

TODAY'S YOUTH COACH

What we have been exploring so far is far from the ideal. We want our coaches to be excellent role models, to teach the skills and mechanics of the game, to exemplify the ideals of good sportsmanship, and to share the love of the game in its traditions and values. Nevertheless, the reality in our communities across the nation is quite different from the ideal for which we strive. Let's take a look.

The Lack of Training

Regardless of the situation, an overwhelming number of coaches have never been trained in the proper ways of teaching kids about sports. And that usually means that disaster is looming just around the corner. I recall one time when I was playing tennis with a friend of mine at a local park, and nearby there was a coach with about fifteen youngsters in what appeared to be one of their first baseball practices of the season.

At the beginning of the practice, the coach decided to hit ground balls to them, and not one child fielded a grounder cleanly. So the ball would roll through their legs or bounce by them, and they'd run and chase it and bring the ball back. I couldn't help but think that this had to be boring for the children and extremely frustrating for the coach.

Then, inexplicably, the coach decided to hit fly balls to

them, when not one of them had mastered grounders yet! He began hitting fly balls, and I'll never forget the looks on the faces of these children. They looked like they were in a war zone and planes were dropping bombs on them from above. They were doing everything they could to dodge the balls so they wouldn't get hit by them.

Shortly thereafter, one of the fly balls bounced off the hood of my car, and I called out to the coach, asking if he could watch out where he was hitting. He didn't waste any time coming over to respond to my request, and as he approached the tennis courts, I was actually relieved that the fence surrounding the courts was separating us because he looked like he was ready to take out his frustrations on me. While I was upset that he had hit my car, I let him know that I was more worried about watching him hit fly balls to these children because they could have been seriously injured.

"So what do you want me to do?" he snapped.

That's the problem. No one had ever told him what he was supposed to do. For all I know, he may have volunteered because no one else was willing to be saddled with the responsibility of coaching this team. Or maybe he thought he'd just rely on how his coaches had taught him when he was growing up. But if volunteers aren't taught the do's and don'ts of coaching, we'll continue to have scenarios like the one above replayed across the country.

These are the individuals who typically don't understand how to organize a practice, know what role winning should play, appreciate how to deal with parents, comprehend what motivates kids, or grasp the important lifetime influence they'll have on children. These adults are in a unique position to impact a child's values, attitudes and ethics, but in the vast majority of programs, they are largely untrained.

While a number of training programs have emerged in recent years, they tend to focus on the mechanics of the game—the X's and O's—without putting any emphasis on what happens when coaches lose perspective, demonstrate poor behavior, or face unanticipated problems.

Winning Isn't Everything

The most misunderstood aspect of youth sports is the role of winning. No matter what I'm discussing on radio, on television, or at a conference, people will usually come away saying that I'm really against competition and winning. Well, nothing could be further from the truth. Winning is what we all must do throughout life to succeed. Getting good grades in school is winning. Being liked by most of the people you know is winning. Being told that you've done a great job at work is winning. Life is full of challenges, and to overcome all of those challenges is winning. Oh, no, I am very much in favor of winning.

Most children want to become involved in sports because they want to have fun, to play. Yet too many coaches have a different view of athletics. They approach the game with only one thought in mind, to win. Thus, the goals of children and their coaches are often quite different.

Soon, the children, being young and impressionable, have their goals warped and distorted by their coaches' attitudes. Sadly, they learn that winning at all costs is acceptable; that cheating is acceptable if you get away with it; that playing injured for the sake of the team is expected; that you're a loser if you're not number one.

If you've attended a youth sports event recently, you know exactly what I mean. The playing fields have become flooded with coaches behaving as if they've just attended a Bobby Knight School of Intimidation. Organized sports have become fertile ground for coaches with bulging veins, foul mouths, clenched fists, and volatile tempers.

These are the coaches who seem to model their behavior after Vince Lombardi's outdated and overused creed, "Winning isn't everything, it's the only thing." This may be fine at the professional level, but totally inappropriate for kids' sports. To illustrate, let me tell a story that demonstrates how we lose perspective about winning.

I'll never forget the time when I was invited to speak at a

conference on youth sports programs for the children of members of the United States military stationed in Korea. During the conference, I attended the championship game of the girls youth softball league. The Northern Division's first place team from Seoul had left their base early that morning for a four-hour bus trip to the site of the championship game. They arrived a little bit late and headed straight out to the field to warm up. But there was a small problem. In their haste to leave, someone had forgotten to pack some of the catcher's equipment.

Immediately, the visiting coach went over to explain that he would need to borrow a catcher's mask and shin guards. It was a simple request; most teams had a couple of spares anyway. But all the home field coach could see was the coveted first place trophy proudly being displayed in his office.

"Just a moment," he said to the visiting coach, and he began to quote from the rule book: "Each team is responsible for bringing its own equipment to the games." Then he read the next rule from the book: "Any team failing to fully equip its players with the mandatory safety equipment must forfeit the game."

The visiting coach looked at him incredulously. He simply could not believe what he was hearing. "Yeah," he said. "That's why I need to borrow a mask and shin protectors, so we can start the game. I'm sure you've got a spare."

The home field coach's only response was to cite the rule book again.

"Look," demanded the visiting coach. "We came a long way this morning. My girls have been working all season long for this. You can't possibly be serious! You can't destroy the hard work of these children over some petty technicality!"

Again the home field coach read from the book in his infuriating tone of voice.

At this point, the exasperated visiting coach walked away to his side of the field, visibly upset, lost as to what to do.

Next, the home field coach brought his rule book to the umpire, showing him a page. At first, the umpire shook his head in disbelief, and then he shrugged his shoulders. Technically, he had to enforce the rules.

Within minutes, the news spread throughout the stands. These were parents and siblings, most for the home team, but some who had made the four-hour trip to see their kids in the championship game. Someone started chanting, "Play the game. Play the game," and pretty soon a lot of the crowd had joined in on the chant. The ten- and eleven-year-olds from the visiting team joined in, and then so did the girls of the home team. They were mutinying against their own coach! They were there for a game and simply wanted to play. They weren't concerned about what the outcome of the game might be.

Humiliated, the coach went out on the field and spoke to the umpire, who turned around and yelled, "Play ball!" A great roar of applause greeted the players as they took the field.

Not that it really matters, but the home team got clobbered that day. The visiting team had been winning their games by substantial margins all year long, and the home field coach probably saw them as unbeatable. The only important thing in his mind was the championship trophy. The fact that twenty or so young people had come to play a game that they had worked hard to prepare for and which was very important to them didn't seem to enter into his thinking. Sportsmanship was irrelevant. Oh, I'm sure there are those who will say a rule is a rule and side with the coach, but these are children's sports where rules should be flexible enough to allow children the rightful chance to play.

The Win-at-All-Costs Mentality

I'm convinced that the classic result of what happens when you turn a group of young athletes over to a coach who has not been given any ethical standards or assistance in applying them, is that the win-at-all-costs philosophy takes over. For some coaches, the notion that there's any other goal involved in youth sports coaching never even dawns upon them. Their every action is guided by a singular principle: What can I do to get my team a win? Forget about developing character, forget about providing a model of good sportsmanship, and forget about whether or not the children are actually having fun. The only thing that matters is having the winning team.

Others begin with noble intentions, but lacking any established standards for the league in which they coach, they find themselves overwhelmed. There may be many unruly kids with all sorts of needs and problems. It's a pretty complicated situation to try to figure out if your concern is for the physical, emotional, and psychological well-being of the entire team. So they eventually do the easy thing, stripping their coaching philosophy down to one simple principle: What do we need to do to win? After all, the whole emphasis presented by the league is to win.

One day, I took my son John and his friend Tommy from the neighborhood down to the local ballpark in Munster, Indiana for baseball try-outs. The fathers who had signed up to participate as coaches were standing around with their clipboards evaluating the skills and performances of the young ball players.

John did fine that day. He had played in youth leagues before and had developed some confidence about his abilities. But it was Tommy's first time playing in front of adults. I had noticed during the drive to the park that he was very nervous about whether he'd perform well enough to make a team. "Just go out there and do your best," I told both of them. But I could see that Tommy was overwhelmed by his nervousness. Not surprisingly, he didn't do very well. When balls were hit to him in the outfield, he missed a lot of them. And because he was a little bit small for his age, he wasn't able to throw the ball all the way into the infield.

It had turned out that there were enough teams to take all the players trying out that year, so that anyone who wanted to play was going to make it onto a team. So the coaches' evaluations were more about whom they wanted on their teams than about deciding who would "make the cut." Tommy looked so depressed by the poor fielding skills he demonstrated that I mentioned to him what I had heard that everyone would get to play that year. "Don't worry about it," I said. "You have the whole year to show them what you're made of."

After his poor performance fielding, Tommy had been identified by a few of the coaches as one of the kids that no one wanted to get stuck with. In disbelief, I listened as they all stood around in a little group gossiping and making jokes amongst themselves when Tommy went up to the plate to demonstrate his hitting abilities. From where I was sitting, I could hear a few of the coaches making a joke over who was going to get "stuck with this kid" on their team. While Tommy couldn't actually hear what the coaches were saying, he could see the way they were looking at him and talking and laughing, so I was pretty sure he got the point.

Each candidate got five pitches to hit, and Tommy swung at each one as if he were trying to knock it out of the park. This was no longer about demonstrating his skills; it was about proving that he wasn't the loser the coaches had labeled him. He missed each of the five pitches, and when he swung at and missed the last one, all the coaches knew who was going to end up being the last pick. One of the coaches then walked over to Tommy, who was still standing at the plate hoping to get another chance to hit the ball. "Thank you, that's enough," he said, and called out the name of the next player.

On the way home from the tryouts, Tommy was pretty depressed, but when I reminded him that it really didn't matter because everyone was going to get to play that year, he seemed to cheer up. He was going to get a whole season to work on his skills and show everyone, especially those coaches, that he could be a competitive player.

But Tommy never really got the chance. The coaches had seen all they needed to see during the tryouts. They never saw the kid who wanted to play and have fun; they never saw the kid who could benefit enormously from developing self-confidence; instead, all they saw was the scrawny kid with limited athletic ability; and they treated him as if his only purpose was to keep the bench warm.

The truth was that Tommy was not the world's worst athlete. My kids said that he was a decent player in pick-up games around the neighborhood. He wasn't the first one picked, but he wasn't the last one, either. They said he was the kind of player who made up for what he lacked in natural ability by playing his guts out. Nevertheless, something apparently had been set in motion during his try-outs that day. From then on, he seemed to have decided that his mission was to prove the coaches wrong and show them he wasn't the loser they had pegged him to be.

For some kids, this sort of pressure can actually be motivational. It enhances their concentration, and they pour all their focus and energy into achieving an exemplary performance. But such kids are the exception to the rule. For most kids, the opposite is true. Instead of the pressure inducing concentration and focus, it creates distraction as they focus not on the moment they're playing in, but on an impossible ideal they're striving for. The result for kids like Tommy is that they tend to perform poorly again and again as they strive to achieve beyond their abilities.

Throughout that first year, the pattern that had been set in motion by the sarcastic attitude of coaches repeated itself over and over again in a vicious circle. Tommy began to feel insecure about the way he was being treated by his coaches and tried to compensate for this insecurity by trying too hard. The saddest thing of all was that there really was a decent athlete, potentially a good athlete underneath his overeager striving. The good athlete was being overrun by his frustration. And so the vicious circle went round and round. Of course, his coach never saw any of this. All he saw was a kid whose athletic performance never made it up to standard, a kid who could not really help with the single-minded goal of winning.

What's the use in expending special energy and attention on a kid who is going to end up riding the bench all season anyway? That seemed to be the attitude of his coach. Perhaps, a coach with a different attitude could have helped Tommy to be the player he wanted to be, but we'll never know.

You see, Tommy finished out the season that year, but he didn't sign up for the league the following year. Sports had become a source of frustration, and so when he got away from it, he never wanted to go back.

A coach's vision on what's best can easily be blurred when the focus begins revolving around the won-lost record. These coaches unforgivably saw Tommy as someone who was only going to hamper the team's success instead of as a child who merely wanted to play a game and develop some skills. Instances such as these occur far too often. Coaches are crossing their own moral boundaries of what's really the right thing to do and surrendering to the winning-is-everything sickness, which can be as addictive to coaches as drugs are to a junkie.

Macho Attitudes

It's truly amazing how the macho attitudes have become a fixture in youth football programs. For the most part, we're talking about regular everyday fathers who, once they arrive at the field and are handed the coaching reins of a youth football team, all of a sudden take on the personality of a drill sergeant. When they're not getting in the face of eight-year-olds who may have dropped a pass or missed a block, they're throwing out absurd clichés like, "No pain, no gain," and, "Be a man, get back in there." A youth football coach somehow thinks that holding that title gives him the license to act like a tough guy because, as one explained it to me, they're coaching a tough sport for tough kids.

I once knew a youth league football coach who would bring a big cooler of beer to the practices, and even some of the games. As the players were warming up on the field before practices, he and his fellow coaches would smoke a few cigarettes and have a few beers while they discussed the players and strategies. From the way they talked, especially after they had a few beers in them, you would have thought that they were coaching a professional sports team.

These were thirteen-year-old kids whose main motivation in signing up for football was to have fun and socialize with their friends. But the head coach turned it into a high pressure situation, doing everything he could to make the kids feel humiliated if they didn't value winning over having fun. Using foul language, he would berate the kids for the simplest mistakes. If he decided that some of his players weren't hustling, he would call them out and make them run laps around the track "to teach them a lesson." And when a player complained about being in pain, he would tell him to "shake it off" and send him back into the action with the words, "Be a man!" The coach justified all of this by imagining that he was producing tough players for a tough game.

During the little pep talks that accompanied the end of each practice, the coaches would naturally focus on the upcoming opponents. There was rarely any talk of giving 100 percent, or doing the best they could. Instead, they talked in violent phrases about "kicking the crap" out of the other team, doing what it takes to "give them a good whipping." During training exercises, the children were taught how to hit and tackle to maximize the opponent's potential for injury, and there were discussions on the fine art of how to hold players without getting flagged by the referee.

In short, these were the types of coaches who took a potentially positive, healthy, fun, character-building activity and turned it into a high-pressure competition where the physical, emotional, and psychological well-being of children took a back seat to a macho-driven desire for a winning team. Without ever seriously considering the effects of their actions on the lives of these children, these men had become responsible for guiding, inspiring, and leading a group of children.

And they were having a negative effect in every single area that should have been positive and fulfilling.

The luckiest kids are the ones whose conscientious and observant parents removed them from the program early on. The other kids in such a situation are those who slowly but surely lose their enthusiasm for participation in organized sports. They aren't having fun, and some are being treated abusively. The likelihood is that the experience will turn a lot of these kids off to organized sports participation all together. Having tried it, and having had an awful experience, they'll never give it a second chance, seeking their needs for self-affirmation, socialization, and self-esteem through other hopefully positive paths in life.

How Safe Are the Coach's Actions?

Sometimes, the coach's actions in search of the Almighty Win can actually be called child abuse. It may not be deliberate; it may amount to ignorance, indifference, or arrogance; but in any event, it puts at risk the safety of the children under his care. See what you think.

Making the Weight

A good friend of mine from Atlanta told me of a mother in the league he was coaching who had gone to her son's football practice to pick him up early for a dentist appointment that she'd forgotten about. When she arrived at the practice, however, she didn't see her son anywhere. She went up to the coach and asked him where her son was. He told her nonchalantly that he was trying to make the weight limit. This happened to be the day when all the players were weighed by the league to make sure that they met the league's weight limits.

"What do you mean he's trying to make the weight limit?" demanded the mother. She had not been informed that her son needed to lose any weight to qualify for the team.

"He's over in my car," the coach admitted. "He's just try-

90

ing to drop a few pounds to make the 98-pound limit. We have weigh-ins tonight."

The mother knew that her son's normal weight was around 105, but when the coach pointed to his car over on the other side of the parking lot, she didn't wait around to ask why he had been placed in the wrong league. She immediately ran toward the car in a state of shock. She found her son sitting in the car wrapped in plastic garbage bags with the engine running and the heater on high.

The coach's plan was to get her son, who was a good running back, down to weight by sweating it off. This goal had completely eclipsed his concern for the welfare of a player. The fact of the matter is that his ignorance and negligence placed a child's health and potentially his life, at risk. Would you not call this child abuse?

Unfortunately, these stories can be read in newspapers across the country virtually on a daily basis. In a 1995 issue of *Sports Illustrated*, there was a frightening account of a youth football coach in the Chicago area who acknowledged that he had given the diuretic Lasix to players as young as ten years old, so they could lose weight and meet the league's weight requirements.

Lack of First-Aid Training

Another serious potential for danger occurs when coaches who know little or nothing about first aid need to deal with the inevitable situation of a child's injuries.

During the early part of my career, all of my experience coaching was at the high school level, where the coaches had some degree of training and education before being given the authority to coach a competitive team. I really didn't know, from first-hand experience, what it was like out there in the world of youth leagues with untrained volunteer coaches. So one day, I decided to find out if the reality was as bad as all the horror stories that were continually circulating around the office where, as I mentioned earlier, I was the youth sports director overseeing programs in Wilmington, Delaware. I would sort of go undercover to find out. I signed up with a youth baseball league outside of my jurisdiction, and it didn't take long for reality to hit home.

During the third inning of one of the first baseball games I coached, the umpire called a time out. The pitcher, who was about nine years old, had been grabbing his arm as if in pain every time he threw the ball. I kept expecting the coach of the other team to stop the game because it was obvious that the youngster's arm was in pretty bad shape, and that he experienced a lot of pain each time he pitched the ball. But the coach of the other team seemed intent on keeping him in, yelling words of "encouragement" out to the mound after every pitch like, "You can do better than that!" or, "Come on, that's not the way I taught you how to throw!"

If the umpire hadn't stopped the game just then, I would have. Clearly, it seemed, the coach of the other team did not have a grasp of the situation.

When the umpire suggested to him that the pitcher appeared to be in pain and that it would be a good idea to replace him, the coach bellowed, "This is my team, and he happens to be my son. I'll decide when it's time to take anybody out of the game."

Then the boy chimed in, "But, dad, my elbow really hurts every time I throw. I don't want to pitch anymore." Then he began to cry.

"This isn't a game for crybabies," said his father. "Now, you get back on the mound and finish the inning."

In disbelief, the players in the dugout and on the field and parents in the stands watched as the little nine-year-old went back to the mound to continue pitching. He wiped tears from his eyes with the back of his baseball glove.

There was no way I was going to sit back and let this happen, so I trotted out to the field in the hopes of helping the umpire talk some sense into this guy.

"There will be other games for him to pitch in," I said to the coach. "If he keeps pitching with his arm in pain like that . . ."

I never got to finish my sentence. He wanted to know "who the hell I thought I was" and then with his index finger pointing toward my chest, he proceeded to let loose a stream of meaningless vulgar language loud enough for everyone to hear. When he was through with his tirade, I took a deep breath and with all the calm I could muster, informed the umpire that our team would be forfeiting the game.

Here was a guy who exhibited abusive behavior toward his own son for all the world to see. But there was nothing that could be done about him. Anyone who wanted to could sign up to be the coach, and as long as he didn't break any laws, he could pretty much do whatever he wanted. It turned out that his son's arm was seriously hurt, and when his kid quit the team, luckily for everyone else, the coach quit, too. We had to quickly recruit a new coach to finish out the year, but I remember my relief knowing that so many young impressionable minds were going to escape the wicked influence of his cruel behavior.

The Need for More Training

It was my experience in the field that convinced me how critical was the role of a volunteer coach, and how important it was for someone to tell coaches that volunteering their time was, in itself, not quite enough. They needed a basic education program that trained them to make sports positive, safe, and fun for kids. Without it, they would lose a tremendous opportunity to do wonders for the team. Without it, they might put their egos first. Without it, they stood a good chance of hurting their youngsters, both psychologically and physically.

I recall a situation that occurred during one of my kid's baseball games. My son David was standing at the plate while his friend Jeff, who had just stolen third base, stood primed to run in for the score. David ripped a line drive that went into and then fell out of the glove of the shortstop, who then scrambled to retrieve the ball. With this, Jeff began his mad dash toward home. It was going to be a very close play. The catcher, reaching for the ball, took a step toward third base as Jeff came barreling toward the plate at top speed. As the ball hit the catcher's glove, Jeff dove head first. But he never got to the plate. His left shoulder and upper arm slammed into the catcher's shin protectors and then were crushed beneath them as the catcher crashed down on top of him.

When Jeff got up, he was holding his arm, hugging it to his chest in obvious pain. His coach led him off the field and told him to rest a while in the dugout. "You'll be okay," he said as Jeff moaned with pain. "Just take it easy on that arm."

Then the coach went back out on to the field and resumed urging his team on as the game continued. I was pretty surprised by this, because from what I had seen of the collision, and the way Jeff was holding his arm, I was pretty sure that some fairly serious damage had occurred.

When I walked down to the dugout, Jeff was in tears from the pain in his arm. The coach was still out urging his team along. When I told the coach that Jeff's arm needed immediate medical attention, he said, "Oh, is it that bad?"

I could tell from the way the bone appeared to be lying against the skin that Jeff might have suffered a compound fracture. When I informed the coach of this, his only comment was, "Oh wow," and he seemed more than content to let me handle the situation as he looked more intently to the play on the field.

I put Jeff's arm on a clipboard so that it could be immobilized, and his mom took him to the hospital. There, they checked it out and confirmed that it was indeed a broken bone. They set it and placed it in a cast.

The following day, I confronted the coach, asking him why he didn't take a more cautious approach to Jeff's injury. After all, this was the coach of my own son.

"Look," he said. "I'm sorry it happened. I volunteered to coach a baseball team, but I never said I was any kind of a doctor."

While it's easy to find fault with the coach for not taking a more responsible attitude toward his player's injuries, it is important to remember that he had no training in how to deal with such situations. So, even if he had done something, it might have done more harm than good.

EVERYONE CAN BE A WINNER

Volunteer youth coaches have the power to turn children off to sports forever, or to make sports a life-long passion. With the proper training, knowledge, and skills, a coach can improve the quality of his children's life immensely and help prepare them for the future. Yet coaches who operate from ignorance can do enormous harm with the same activity. We can't insure that every coach will do what's best for children in every case, but we can adopt policies requiring that every coach has at least been exposed to a good training program before he coaches a child.

Most coaches volunteer with a kind heart and with the best of intentions. They have no desire to do anything other than what's best for all the kids. But far too many have never been shown how. Given what's at stake, the quality of our children's lives, shouldn't we insist that coaches know how to make sports a fun, supportive, healthy experience for kids? Furthermore, shouldn't we have a mechanism to remove the abusers, the intimidators, and the incompetents?

Coaches have an important responsibility to provide effective guidance and instruction in the techniques and strategies of their sport and to create a psychologically healthy setting in which children can derive the positive benefits of sports participation. If we can create this type of atmosphere, then everyone can become a winner, regardless of the won-lost record at the end of the season. What children will carry away with them from their sports experiences will endure far longer than the outcome of any single contest.

Later, we'll detail proven solutions that have helped volunteer coaches across the country do what's best for the children on their teams. First, however, we need to examine the role of the sports administrator.

CHAPTER FIVE

Administrators—
The Key to It All

In this chapter, we're going to shift the spotlight away from the playing field, shine it behind the scenes, and examine those who can enact the policies, implement the changes, and alter the rules to benefit all of the young athletes, as well as their parents, coaches, and officials. We will take a look at the administrators of our youth sports programs. After all, if they use their resources properly, they have the ability to leave a lasting positive effect on the programs under their care and lay a strong foundation for an enjoyable experience for all.

Yet too many administrators, despite the best of intentions, are clearly in over their heads as they deal with a tidal wave of issues that engulf them. These concerns may vary from financial management to recruiting volunteers, from fund-raising to safety, from gender issues to establishing and maintaining a philosophy for the league. With such a wide range of problems and issues on their agendas, the administrators must be very special kinds of people.

WHAT DO WE EXPECT OF OUR ADMINISTRATORS?

A good place to start would be to ask what we expect of the people who assume the role of administrator of a youth league in our community. Most people would say that they would fulfill four major functions:

1. **Operations.** Administrators should see to the day-to-day operations of the league—things like scheduling games, finding good coaches, assigning umpires, securing playing fields, and the like.

2. **Enforcing policies.** Administrators should require that the league's policies be enforced—such things as age limits, playing time, rules interpretation, and weather conditions—all of which affect the games and how they are played.

3. **Financial management.** Administrators must account for the funds, purchase the uniforms and equipment, and keep track of the inventory.

4. **Ceremonial functions.** Administrators should preside at the opening day ceremonies, all-star games, and playoffs. They should also present trophies and awards.

In many respects, therefore, people think of youth athletic administrators in the same way they think of company presidents. After all, they are also in charge of planning, budgeting, staffing, and inventory; they present awards and plaques for a job well done. However, as we will discuss below, the role of the youth sports administrator is far more complicated than scheduling, financing, and playing emcee.

Not a Company President

The differences between the company president and the youth sports administrator are enormous. Administrators of youth sports programs across the country are just like you and me. Having been a high school athletic director, I have a deep respect for these people and applaud their dedication. They may be carpenters, teachers, executives, store owners, you name it, but largely, they're everyday people who have full-

98

time jobs and have volunteered their free time to run a youth league in their community. We expect them to take charge and act in the best interests of the children. And that represents the greatest difference between the company president and the youth sports administrator: The company president usually deals with manufactured products, and the sports administrator deals with children. And that's a huge contrast.

A second major difference is in the degree of training between the two individuals. The business leader usually has had specialized training, earned a college degree, probably in business, attended conferences, and learned through years of experience. Youth sports administrators, on the other hand, are typically sincere and caring individuals who have the best of intentions in taking over the reins of a program. After all, they're sacrificing an enormous amount of time and energy to fill these positions. Some may even have vigorously pursued the position or perhaps were encouraged by others to take over. However, regardless of how they got the post, they can be easily overwhelmed by the enormity of the issues, concerns, and problems they face. Even if they had been top-notch high school athletes or talented enough to play in college, they may not have the credentials to administer a youth sports program; after all, the talents and skills required for playing a sport and administering a league are quite different.

Risky Assumptions

Parents must make sure that their children are in good hands, but most caring parents don't have the slightest idea who the person is heading up the local youth league. Since the program is run at the local recreation department field, parents take it for granted that the people who run the leagues are well qualified. Nevertheless, I would venture to say that most of the thousands of volunteer parents who head up these programs have little understanding of such issues as the effects of early maturation on athletic performance, safety and the prevention of injuries, recruiting and training volunteers, and financial accountability, among others.

Sure, most of our youth program administrators are volunteers, not highly trained, experienced corporate presidents. But we are not talking about a manufactured product here; we're talking about our precious children, youngsters who are developing physically, mentally, emotionally, and socially.

In most cases, what parents expect of their league administrators is not what they get. Because many parents simply don't realize the serious psychological, emotional, and mental effects sports have on our children, they play Russian roulette when they casually trust their offspring to the local league. They simply enroll their children, drop them off at the field, and assume that the experience meets their needs. They see kids hitting, kicking, catching, running, and throwing, and assume it is play for them, assume it is safe for them, assume they are in good hands.

However, I believe, with the welfare of our precious children at stake, these are dangerous assumptions, for the reverse is too often true. Let me give you an example.

Several years ago, I attended a meeting of almost thirty presidents of youth sports leagues at a conference. I showed them an award-winning video called *Winning Is Everything*, produced by Barton Cox Productions in California. I wanted them to see the ugly side of sports administration, because in the film, there were scenes of coaches who were belittling kids, physically abusing them, and worse. It was a total indictment of the way their leagues' sports programs were being administered.

As the video ended, I anticipated a negative backlash and prepared for the worst. After all, the message of this video was that the programs the administrators were supervising were very damaging to kids.

There was a strange silence in the room as the last scene appeared on the screen. It was almost scary. Then one of the league presidents looked at all his counterparts at the table and, with a strong voice of commitment, stated, "There's not a damn one of you sitting at this table that doesn't know that this kind of situation goes on in all our programs every day." No one said a word. It seemed like they were too embarrassed to talk.

In all reality, this experience was the major boost that I desperately needed at the time. It told me the problems were not local or regional, but national. It told me to move forward, to fight to change the system. I had hit a nerve, and I was inspired to do even more until every leader had heard the message. Here were almost 30 adults who collectively influenced the lives of more than 10,000 children saying that there was something very harmful about what they were doing.

TYPES OF ADMINISTRATORS

Before we can fully understand the actions of our administrators, we need to first understand just who these people are and how they came to occupy their current positions of influence. The majority, of course, are volunteers, but there are also those who are, in fact, "professionals." Let's take a closer look at both types.

The Volunteer

Volunteer administrators historically only follow in the footsteps and maintain the guidelines of those who preceded them. If the league has high standards and a no-nonsense policy to eliminate abusive behavior among coaches and parents, then they follow in that tradition. If the league is run by a group of win-at-all-cost, diehard individuals, they follow in that tradition. No one rocks the boat; the status quo rules; change is discouraged. Psychologically, the volunteers do not feel equipped to take on the "establishment" and attempt change, especially if the suggested improvements are broad and fundamental.

The Professional

The other type of administrator is the professional in parks and recreation departments, Boys and Girls Clubs, YMCAs, church organizations, and military recreation for dependent families. I have great respect for these groups of people, as it is they who have helped our association train over a million volunteer coaches. But even with this group, there is often a glaring lack of knowledge about how to improve and become more effective.

A few years after I had founded the NYSCA, I was invited to conduct a seminar regarding youth coach training for U.S. Army youth sports administrators in Washington, D.C. There were close to 100 people from Army bases throughout the world. At the conclusion of the session, one of the attendees, Frank Eckhardt, approached me and said, "You know, while it's great that you are focusing on coaches, the real truth of the matter is that you've got it all backwards. The people who really need training and certification are the people you're looking at in this room, myself included, who don't know a thing about running youth sports programs."

Frank knew what he was talking about since he had been the youth sports director at Fort Bragg in North Carolina for several years. As I traveled to military bases around the world, I would see people given the job and title of youth sports director who were hired simply because they were former military athletes or wives of military officers, as well as a few people who had degrees distantly related to organizing and administering youth sports. Most of these people, I must say, craved knowledge about the area because they were, for the most part, sincere, dedicated people. I've seen the same scenario in parks and recreation departments, Boys and Girls Clubs, and virtually every professional organization offering organized sports for children.

THE NEED FOR TRAINING

It would seem we place little value on those who organize

and administer athletic programs for America's youth. If the "professionals" admit even they need training, can we say it is any better for the "volunteers"?

Recently, our Alliance organization commissioned an important national study of 320 youth sports administrators. Our research uncovered some pretty disturbing facts. One major finding is that more than 50 percent of local program administrators don't have *any type* of organizational training. Are you surprised? It also discovered that 83 percent had the power to choose which programs to run; 65 percent, to establish program principles and define the philosophy of the program; and 68 percent, to develop the policies and regulations for their programs. You can see that these administrators exercise a great deal of "power," implementing programs that have a profound effect on our children's physical, emotional, social, and mental development. Yet they are, for the most part, volunteers with no training!

I know our youth league administrators want to succeed. They have told me so in my meetings with them across the nation. I fully believe they would be much better equipped to handle the varied problems in youth athletics if they were adequately trained to do so.

PROBLEMS ADMINISTRATORS FACE

The evident need for administrator training is just one major problem the Alliance and I have identified. Using the results of our national Alliance survey, in addition to our more than three decades of experience in the field, we have identified eight significant issues facing league administrators:

1. Keeping the organization's philosophy focused on the participants

2. Managing the league finances

3. Raising funds to support the programs

4. Recruiting volunteers

Officials

One of the major problems administrators face is finding qualified officials to interpret the action on the field or in the arena, control the game, enforce the rules, and make sure the players, the coaches, and the game are treated with respect.

Officiating in youth sports programs presents some unique problems. What typically happens is that leagues and organizations rely either on teenagers who have played the game and "sorta" know the rules, or on moms and dads who are coaxed into officiating at games when no one else is available. Just think how often you've seen dad picked out of the stands to come down and umpire first base. It happens all the time. But without understanding the true meaning of sports, these volunteers can fall into the same trap that many coaches do. They begin officiating at games in the same manner they see done at the high school, college, and professional level.

So what's wrong with that? For starters, officials play just as important a role in the youth sports setting as coaches, parents, and administrators. Many people fail to realize that there's so much more to officiating at a youth sports game than simply calling balls and strikes, throwing penalty flags, or whistling fouls. If their words and actions end up hurting children instead of helping them, they can quickly drain the fun out of sports. If children learn to dislike officials at such an early age or distrust their judgment, this attitude can stick with them throughout their athletic careers and create a negative atmosphere.

There's enormous pressure and stress on officials to perform to perfection. As one veteran umpire told me, "It's the only occupation where you must be perfect

> beginning on day one—and every time thereafter."
> These types of expectations are totally unrealistic and
> serve to create all sorts of problems that have become
> an inherent part of organized sports.
>
> In Chapter 7, we'll touch on some ideas for helping
> officials get treated with the respect they deserve, and
> for alleviating many of the other problems that encom-
> pass youth sports officiating.

5. Clarifying the role of girls in youth sports

6. Clarifying the role of disabled youngsters

7. Emphasizing the importance of safety

8. Clarifying the concept of winning

Let's examine each of the issues to see how they influence youth sports programs, in general, and their administrators, in particular.

Philosophy: Focus on Kids

Most national youth sports organizations have wonderful mission statements that clearly define what they are striving to achieve. The problem is that by the time they get down to the local level, these objectives have been abandoned by coaches and parents who are caught up with the win-at-all-costs attitudes so prevalent these days. Consequently, the well-crafted mission statement that sounds nice and looks good in print is never actually implemented at the local level.

I recall a meeting I had with an administrator in a program called the Florida Junior Major League. He told me at season's end there was one person from their district who was assigned to be the "talent recruiter." His job was to travel throughout the district to look over the best players from other teams so that eventually they would have the very best all-star team possible to represent the district. He said he was sure no other district did this, but it was their way to stack the all-star team with the best available talent.

Was this an acceptable philosophy approved by the league headquarters? I am sure it was not, but this is the result when poorly trained administrators accept the status quo and fail to emphasize the appropriate philosophy. Winning becomes the rule, and leagues lose sight of their real mission.

While our Alliance organization was just getting off the ground a few years ago, I went on a promotional trip to Louisiana and visited one of the larger youth leagues in the state. They had a beautiful facility built by the parents and a nice clubhouse for meetings. I couldn't help but notice that the concession stand featured a beer tap with a well-known brewery label. I asked the administrator if they actually sold beer here while the kids played. He said that they did, that beer sales were, in fact, their biggest moneymaker.

"But doesn't that kind of send a bad message to these kids?"

"No," he said. "We've been doing this for years. Things only get out of hand once in a while—when we have a big game."

It's easy to see how the philosophy of those who organize a youth sports league can get lost when the wrong people take over, or when they lose focus on what youth sports are all about. Leadership means standing up for what's right, not caving in to the "winning" philosophy or to increased beer sales. We need administrative leadership.

Financial Management

It is not unusual for a youth league run by volunteers to have a budget that exceeds $100,000. That's a lot of money for anyone to control effectively, and I can't tell you how many times

I have been told stories about administrators who have mismanaged funds. Some of the time, it was just plain incompetence or lack of proper training, but other times, it was dishonesty.

One administrator who had just been elected president of the youth league told me one of the first things he discovered when he took over was how significant funds from the concession stands were missing, and there was no way to account for the money. It seems those "volunteers" running the concession stands pocketed their own little "share" each evening, and there was no way to prove who was guilty and who was not.

I'm sure most people are honest when collecting funds for youth league operations, but administrators still need assistance in ways to prevent theft, to track inventory and equipment, and to acquire the accounting skills necessary to effectively manage large sums of money. We need administrative leadership to make that happen.

Fund-Raising—The Money Pot

Associated with the general concern about financial management is the problem of raising funds to support the athletic program. While schools and professional youth organizations such as Boys and Girls Clubs, YMCAs, and YWCAs have budgets within their systems, parent-run youth leagues must often rely heavily on fund-raising activities to maintain their programs. Organizing candy sales, car washes, raffles, carnivals, and sponsorships are all part of the everyday life of the youth sports administrator—and how many have been trained in these areas? Because registration fees barely cover the costs associated with running a league, administrators need the special fund-raisers to help them to buy the trophies, pay the umpires, procure the uniforms, and purchase the equipment to function properly.

To put that in perspective, let me relay a statistic from a friend who worked for World's Finest Chocolates, one of the nation's biggest fund-raisers. He told me his sales annually exceeded $500,000, just for the local leagues. That's a lot of candy, and our administrators are responsible for it.

It takes a lot of organization to raise the funds needed, and a special group of people to make that happen. However, it seems to me, it also takes some specialized training in financial management, accountability, and fund-raising to make it successful for all involved. This won't happen by itself; we need administrative leadership.

Recruiting Volunteers

Organized youth sports simply would not exist without people volunteering their time to coach, officiate, act as team parents, operate concession stands, and undertake all the other tasks required to operate a successful league. In brief, youth leagues are much like civic and fraternal organizations. The difference is that most parents volunteer because their child is involved in the program, and they feel an obligation to help. For many parents, their volunteer work becomes a time-consuming part of their lives that they won't easily forget.

While attracting volunteers is an important issue, there has always been a myth that, because people are unpaid volunteers, they won't accept the idea of being trained. Nothing could be farther from the truth. My experience is that people actually want to do a good job, and they will gladly accept training. In fact, when they receive no training, they are disappointed and place less value on the position. Worse, when we offer them no training, we create unrealistic expectations—and actually invite tragedy.

The solution seems obvious, if only some intelligent administrators would exercise some leadership. Hundreds of youth leagues now *require* volunteer training and boast how the quality of their leagues has improved. In order to make sports positive, fun, and safe for our children, all leagues should mandate training for their volunteers. To make that happen, we need administrative leadership.

Girls and Sports

It borders on the ludicrous that we even have to spend time explaining why girls should be allowed to play the same sports as boys. In my view, they should be allowed to play any sport, any time, anywhere. Unfortunately, there are many adults who are putting up resistance when it comes to allowing girls to play on the same team as boys or to even play certain sports that have traditionally been male-dominated, such as hockey. It's truly hard to fathom how any reasonable adult would want to deprive any girl of the many benefits of sports. While we've come a long way, we haven't apparently come far enough.

In fact, the gender issue can become the administrators' biggest problem because emotions typically run high on both sides. On one side, you've usually got the parents—and child who wants an opportunity to play—and on the other side, the traditionalists who argue there's no room for girls. Altogether, this can be a sticky situation, with the administrators trapped in the middle.

Every youth league has certain guiding principles that have been established, as well as rules and policies that have been followed to some degree since the league came into existence. These are the rules that are basically carried out and enforced under the interpretation of the administrators. So when it comes to gender, the administrators may have inherited an existing program where girls have never been allowed to play. Consequently, what happens is that these leaders, fearful of initiating any changes, simply run the program as it's always been run. So the vicious cycle of slamming the door of opportunity in the faces of young girls is perpetuated.

Also, the majority of today's male administrators, who may have played sports themselves as children, probably never participated with girls. So during their developmental years, they may have developed socialized prejudices that now affect an entirely new generation of youngsters.

Yet this is where the administrators can take charge, for the responsibility to insure gender equality falls squarely on their shoulders. Girls should not be denied the right to participate in any sport, at any level, so it is up to the responsible administrator to recommend changes, rewrite policies, and suggest improvements to the league's board of directors. These actions must be in the best interests of every young participant—not just the boys.

Should girls be permitted to play sports that have traditionally been reserved for boys? I recently received a letter from a mother in Montgomery, Alabama who wrote that there was never a problem for her two sons to play baseball, but when their little sister tried to follow in their footsteps, gender discrimination reared its ugly head: "Although only seven years old, she was told she belonged on the softball field. The team manager made it obvious he didn't want a female on his team, and his treatment toward her was terrible. The interesting thing is that she moved to another team where she proved to be better than most of the other male players on the team."

Luckily, this little girl's story had a happy ending, but this youngster never should have had to move to another team in the first place. Her treatment by the team manager was disgraceful, and the league administrator should have stepped in and enforced the league's gender discrimination policies. Administrators of sports programs must incorporate an inclusive philosophy when it comes to girls and sports. And that takes leadership.

A Role for the Disabled

Children and adults with disabilities are much more visible in today's society than they have been at any other time in our history. Inclusion has emerged as an important concept in the education of children with special needs, but few administrators recognize and understand this point. We have seen the need for administrators to support inclusive policies regarding girls in sports, and we find a similar need when it comes to children with disabilities.

Including kids with disabilities in activities with their peers who are not disabled is a guiding principle of the Americans with Disabilities Act (ADA), which applies to 43 million people. This 1990 federal law provides an opportunity to welcome all children into youth sports.

The ADA is an important piece of broad-sweeping civil rights legislation that insures the rights of people with disabilities to be included in all aspects of community life, enjoy the full benefits of participation, and be served in the least restricted setting.

Youth league administrators must remember that kids with disabilities are, first and foremost, children. These youngsters have the same dreams and desires as others do. The only difference is that they happen to have a condition that may affect some of their abilities and skills, but that doesn't mean that they shouldn't be able to reap the benefits that sports provide. So their participation in the youth sports arena should be fully supported by everyone involved, not because of any law, but because it's the right thing to do.

The adults should be removing roadblocks to participation, not putting them in. Many youth leagues have policies and mission statements that at least touch on the goal of helping children learn and develop skills for that particular sport, among other areas. Administrators must realize that all children have a right to learn and develop these skills to the best of their ability.

Born without a right hand, former pitcher Jim Abbott played Major League baseball with only one "good" arm. In fact, one year, he pitched a no-hitter for the New York Yankees. Abbott is wonderful proof that if given the opportunity, anyone can excel, regardless of the limitations adults may perceive a child to have.

Why should a child who has a speech impediment, a learning disorder, a vision problem, or a physical ailment be denied one of life's greatest treasures—the chance to partici-

The Power of Title IX

Prior to 1970, if a woman wanted to pursue an advanced degree in college, chances were she wouldn't be admitted to a law school or medical school program, simply because she was a woman. Unfortunately, that's just one of many sad reminders of the cruel behaviors that have left a nasty scar on American history. However, in 1972, Congress passed Title IX of the 1972 Education Amendments Act, a federal law that prohibits discrimination on the basis of gender at educational institutions that accept federal funds. Popularly called Title IX, this law opened the door for more women to become doctors, lawyers, and college athletes.

Title IX also applies to junior high schools and high schools, where young female participants should receive the same treatment as their male counterparts. Despite the law, this is not always the case. Reports continue to surface about institutions across the country that are failing to live up to the Title IX requirements. We see some of those very same problems in youth sports, as well.

Nevertheless, because of Title IX, we have made progress in the area of gender equality. More girls are participating in organized sports than ever before—and at earlier ages. A massive gender revolution is occurring, and it has far-reaching implications. A virtual army of young girls will grow up competing with boys in some sports, developing social skills, and building self-esteem in an arena that most of their mothers never knew. I believe this will eventually manifest itself in more assertive and confident adult women in the workplace as this generation matures. A new social dynamic is unfolding, one that threatens to demolish every preconceived assumption of how women are supposed to act under pressure.

It is imperative that league administrators also support Title IX and gender equality—as long as administrators don't throw up roadblocks by running programs in an old-fashioned manner just because they "don't believe girls belong," or because "this is how it's always been run."

According to research from the Women's Sports Foundation, half of all girls who participate in some kind of athletics develop higher than average levels of self-esteem, and they experience less depression than girls who are not active in sports. Later, as teenagers, girls who have high self-esteem are less likely to become pregnant, and, as adults, are more likely to leave an abusive relationship than girls with low self-esteem. When teenagers evaluate themselves in a positive way, they are more capable of avoiding drugs, alcohol, tobacco, gangs, and violence. Of course, high self-esteem will not guarantee that youngsters will always make responsible decisions, but it does provide a stronger basis for resisting the pressures that currently exist in society today. Now, because of Title IX, that is more likely to be the case for all the youth of America, male *and* female.

pate in sports? And why do so many administrators cruelly continue to step on these youngsters' dreams by turning them away season after season? It's because winning championships and trophies are the main goals in the minds of many administrators, even though in the process, some youngsters are excluded. It's time administrators began to put aside their petty prejudices, ignore their fears of the unknown, become better informed on these issues, and educate the coaches and parents throughout the league who have a responsibility, as decent human beings, to welcome *all* children to the world of youth athletics.

Injuries—More Than We Think

Administrators often come into their position thinking that in any given season a certain number of children are going to get hurt. They'll tell themselves it's all part of the game. In their minds, the sprained ankles, broken arms, twisted knees, and blackened eyes become the accepted price children have to pay to play sports. With the long hours administrators put in and all the time they're forced to spend wrestling with budgets, the last thing many really think about is safety. Most administrators would never think that the decisions they make on something they perceive as inconsequential—like purchasing a new catcher's mask—could actually result in a child losing the use of an eye. And that's where problems begin.

Prior to the 1970s, overuse injuries—those caused by repetititive stress—were virtually unheard of, but with the emergence of longer seasons, sports camps, and more intensive training, doctors are diagnosing more of these injuries nationwide. The reason? Children participating in organized leagues are being urged to throw just one more pitch, to run just one more lap, or stay on the field to tackle just one more opponent. Sports medicine experts say they are seeing more serious injuries, more injuries from overuse, more girls getting hurt, and more younger kids getting injured while participating in sports.

Children are concentrating on one sport at younger and younger ages, and playing that sport year-round, using the same groups of muscles again and again. Some kids may be more susceptible than others to overuse injuries because their muscles may not be developed fully enough to handle repetitive activities, placing extra stress on ligaments and tendons.

In my view, it is inexcusable for administrators to subject children to unnecessary risks that could be prevented by a common-sense approach. One of the major problems occurs when children with minimal skills and coordination are required to use equipment that is appropriate only for serious

Meeting the Challenge: Buddy Ball

Each year, the National Youth Sports Coaches Association selects a Coach of the Year from among approximately 150,000 volunteer youth coaches nationwide. The 1995 recipient was Beth Campbell of Bellevue, Washington, who was hailed as an "angel of mercy" in the flood of nomination letters that poured in from parents who have embraced her efforts. Because Beth couldn't stand to see disabled children missing out on the fun and excitement of playing with their peers, she developed "Buddy Ball," a truly special approach to youth sports.

Buddy Ball is a variation on T-ball. It includes a big dose of heart, encouragement, and kindness, but it still allows the thrill of competition. In this game, physically and mentally challenged youngsters from kindergarten through fifth grade are paired with normally developed children who do for their partners what they can't do for themselves. For example, a child with cerebral palsy who is confined to a wheelchair still gets the chance to bat and then is pushed around the bases by a teammate. Or a youngster with Down's syndrome is helped by a teammate to catch and throw a ball in the outfield.

Beth got the idea for Buddy Ball when she took her then seven-year-old son Stevie, who is nonverbal, to watch his older brother Chris play baseball. She realized how desperately he also wanted to have fun and play. In the past, kids like Stevie would have been banished to teams for the handicapped that further isolated them, but now, with Buddy Ball, they can be part of a normal team environment.

At our Coach of the Year awards ceremony, Beth delivered a riveting acceptance speech that brought more than a few people to tears. She talked about how

Stevie and other challenged kids on the team who are around regularly-developed kids are encouraged to strive harder to reach their maximum abilities: "All children want to do their best, and any child can, if given the opportunity. Inside, they're just like you and me. Participating side by side and not in separate programs makes a great difference, in that kids without disabilities learn to see beyond the outside to the spirit within. The disabled may not be as talented in the same ways," she continued, "but they are just as valuable. Our challenge is to find ways to involve and develop every child."

Those challenging comments to the audience made a lot of sense to me, and I felt pretty proud that night knowing that our organization, through our National Coach of the Year award, had given Beth a platform to present a fresh perspective on inclusion.

However, that feeling of pride was soon swept away as I stood in the lobby following the break. I overheard two gentleman, apparently league administrators, discussing the issue as others milled about. I remember one saying, "If you think I'm going to allow these kind of kids in our league, you're crazy. This isn't what sports is about. It's like they think we're some kind of social agency or something."

The mentality demonstrated by these two individuals spoke volumes about the sad attitudes many youth league administrators exhibit across the country. Their focus is on winning the local, regional, state, and national championships, and that means weeding out those less talented. In their misguided view, that includes the handicapped.

Buddy Ball takes the opposite point of view: Every kid gets to play, the score isn't the focus, and innings aren't over until everyone gets a turn at bat. Everybody plays—and as seen by all the smiling faces—everybody is a winner.

In my view, Buddy Ball should be a part of every league, every sport—and every administrator's vocabulary. To make that happen, we need administrative leadership.

competitions among athletes with well-developed skills and coordination.

Nowhere is this more dramatic than in the instance of children using hard balls in youth baseball leagues. In Major League baseball, the only death that ever resulted from a pitched ball occurred in 1920 when widely-hated New York Yankee pitcher Carl Mays beaned popular Cleveland Indians shortstop Ray Chapman. However, in youth baseball, death has become sadly much more common. In fact, according to the Consumer Product Safety Commission, baseball is the leader in youth sports fatalities. Why? Because children have not established the motor skills of eye tracking, coordination, and timing to avoid being hit by a hard ball being pitched or hit by a batter. Administrators are often quick to claim that baseball is safer than riding a bike or the countless other activities children do on a daily basis. But try telling that to the parents across the country who have lost a son or daughter on the playing field.

I recall reading a study, released by the Consumer Product Safety Commission, that detailed the deaths of children who had been killed during baseball and softball games. The following are some examples:

- An eight-year-old was hit in the chest by a pitched ball and suffered cardiac arrest during an organized game in Illinois.

- Another eight-year-old boy was struck on the chest by a pitch during batting practice immediately preceding a Little League game. He died of cardiac arrest.

- A nine-year-old in Pennsylvania was struck in the right lateral area of the chest during an organized game. Although a qualified nurse was present and started CPR immediately, no blood could get to the victim's brain. The child was, in fact, brain dead.

- A fourteen-year-old Indiana boy died while in surgery after being hit on the left side of the head with a pitched baseball. He was not wearing a protective batting helmet.

According to a report released by the National Youth Sports Safety Foundation utilizing data from the Consumer Product Safety Commission, more than twenty children were killed participating in organized baseball and softball games between 1973 and 1994. Furthermore, annually, more than 190,000 youngsters under the age of fifteen require a trip to the hospital emergency room for injuries sustained while participating in organized football, basketball, baseball, and soccer programs. Note that those numbers don't take into account all the other sports that youngsters play.

The administrator's first question must be, "What policy is best for the *children?*" And the first task must be to insure that the children are playing in the safest environment possible. The administrator must constantly ask, "Have I done everything within my power to reduce the chance of injury?"

League administrators are not going to be able to stop all accidents from happening, but they can take steps to insure that safety is a high priority, that safety equipment is in place, that officials enforce safety rules, and that safety recommendations are given careful consideration.

But safety considerations should go beyond the game itself. There are other factors that a lot of administrators have probably never even considered. For example, how many administrators ever check out the safety of the area surrounding the field? If the field is near a busy street or highway, there should be consideration given to having a crossing guard present so children aren't in danger coming to and going from games. And what about the field itself? Is there an established policy for inspecting the playing area for loose rocks, holes in the ground, broken glass, or any other types of debris that could injure a child? The same holds true for indoor sports. The court needs to be inspected for wet spots where a child could slip during the course of play. There are so many safety issues that somehow they get pushed into the background when they should be at the top of every administrator's list.

Yes, to some degree accidents are going to happen in organized sports, but we can't accept arrogance or negligence. Of course, lax administrators risk lawsuits, but more important, they risk the welfare of the children entrusted to their care. Instead, they must act decisively and do whatever it takes to make youth sports as safe as possible for every participant. They need to exercise strong leadership.

Is Winning the Primary Objective?

As we've already established, the majority of administrators either aren't adequately qualified or lack the necessary training to do an effective job. Thus, what often happens is that these individuals rely on the example of the professional leagues.

I can't help but think that's why we've seen the emergence of drafts for youth league team sports. For example, I have seen a youth football league in which all the kids who have signed up to play show up at a field on a Saturday morning and are asked to throw, catch, and run pass patterns. Meanwhile, all of the coaches, armed with their clipboards and stopwatches, scribble data on their notepads, in hopes they will be able to draft the best players for their team. It has all the makings of the National Football League's annual "scouting combine" where rookies are tested by coaches and

119

general managers—they throw passes, run pass patterns, and execute forty-yard dashes—except that *our* participants can be as young as six or seven years old.

Children at these ages shouldn't be forced into these stressful situations where how they perform is all that matters. It's going to be a pretty traumatic experience for children who drop a pass in front of a whole group of coaches whom they desperately want to impress. And why were they put into this position in the first place? Only because all they wanted to do was play a sport and have fun in the process.

The days when you could go and sign up with your buddy and be guaranteed that you'd get to play on the same team are rapidly disappearing. Now it's about who can corral the best players for their team, even if it means splitting up friends who were looking forward to playing together.

Furthermore, many communities have embraced "select teams," a dangerous precedent that is already wreaking havoc. These are the programs that promote winning as the primary objective and that encourage only the very best players to play, while the less talented ones sit idly by on the bench, only getting in the game when another youngster gets injured.

A *Dayton Daily News* article examined a select team basketball league of third graders. In the story, one of the coaches is quoted as saying, "We don't want to lose a ballgame because we played kids equally. It's sort of like a business: I'm trying to put the best product out on the floor."

The story quoted another coach as saying, "If the other team is playing to win, you pretty much have to, as well."

You can hardly blame the coaches. Their league philosophy actually rewards this type of behavior. This particular basketball league even went so far as to put its philosophy down in writing and distribute it to the parents. It said, in part, "While the commitment of [the league] is to develop talent, the parents and players must realize that [the league] will play to win. . . . There is no guarantee regarding playing time."

Do you remember Bill Hughes and his "Everybody Plays" philosophy? Do you remember Grantland Rice and his idea, "It's how you play the game"? Can you see how far we have strayed from those ideals? Can you see how the game has changed—for the worse? Can you see how the youth sports league administrators have "gone along" with those who would unwittingly ruin the game?

Our children deserve better. It is our task to return the game to them. In accomplishing that task, we need administrative leadership.

A HIGHER STANDARD

The very values we can learn through organized sports— things such as ethics, fair play, sportsmanship, and teamwork—are the lessons that will guide us to be the best we can in life. One could argue that what we learn on the ballfield is as important as what we learn in the classroom. And this is the reason that those who head youth athletic organizations should be held to a higher set of standards.

As you have seen, administrators play an enormously important role in our youth sports programs. They are the lifelines of these programs. The decisions they make, the manner in which they choose to enforce rules, and the ways they implement change—or not—will all leave a permanent imprint on the children who participate in their leagues. We desperately need their leadership.

CHAPTER SIX

Return the Game to the Children

It's amazing what so many of today's children endure in the so-called name of fun while participating in organized sports. Yes, there are a great many sincere, dedicated adults out there who have the kids' best interests at heart. Yet, as we've discussed in the preceding chapters, there are also many adults who have helped to produce an army of children who don't feel so good about themselves because they've had a negative sports experience. In this chapter, however, we're not going to examine the adults; we're going to look at the results of the adults' actions on the children.

Yes, there are some pretty terrific programs, some pretty terrific people, but there are also some pretty compelling numbers released over the years from a variety of national studies that paint a disturbing picture of children's reactions to programs and adults that are not so terrific. One major finding: Because of a variety of reasons, seven out of ten children will quit organized sports before they reach their thirteenth birthday. Another: If a girl does not participate in sports by the time she is ten, there is less than a 10-percent chance that she will be participating when she is twenty-five years old. Another: A staggering number of children will wind up in hospital emergency rooms with sports injuries, many of which could have been prevented. I believe these kinds of problems are happening nationwide because many adults fail to see the game from the child's point of view. And the consequences—as we've seen far too often—are disastrous.

One major problem is that many adults misunderstand the whole concept of *play*. On the surface, play may *seem* like a pretty simple subject. Nevertheless, the simple act of playing is often confused with *competition*, an allied idea we'll also explore. We'll take a serious look at why many children actually fear competition, examine why children are quitting sports in such numbers, and share some heartbreaking stories of some who have suffered irreparable damage on the playing fields. We will examine two issues—burnout and sports injuries—that have been largely neglected. Finally, we'll look at a fundamental idea that may actually surprise most parents—many children simply aren't ready for organized sports.

CONFUSING PLAY WITH COMPETITION

When children are five, six, or seven years old, many parents have a strong impulse to guide them down a successful path in life. There's nothing wrong, of course, with wanting the best for our kids. But problems develop when we set goals for our kids without carefully taking into account the reality of a child's nature, without seeing the world from the child's point of view. A typical case is that of parents who, anxious to imagine their children on the fast track to superstardom, forget that children are just children.

As a former physical education teacher at the elementary school level, I know how important playing is in the life of a healthy child. After all, it is the most natural of acts and provides children with the chance to learn independence, develop self-esteem, and explore their physical abilities. But parents can rob children of this important outlet if they are not aware of the enormous benefits that children derive through play.

The Concept of Play

It's critical that we as parents understand the significant difference between *play* and *competition*. Without knowing the difference, we risk pushing our children too hard, destroying their self-confidence, and damaging their self-esteem. In the process, we take away the number one objective of play—fun.

So just what is play?

Play covers everything from amusement to exercise to diversion. It is almost anything we do that is just for fun. It provides mental and physical amusement with the motive being enjoyment, relaxation, and stress-free pleasure.

Let's go one step further and take a moment to explore the meaning of play with these four questions:

1. When the umpire at a T-ball game says, "Play ball," are children playing?

2. When a child is building a sandcastle, is she playing?

3. When your son is standing at the free-throw line of a tied basketball game with two seconds left, is he playing?

4. When your nine-year-old daughter is feverishly working the controls of her Nintendo game, is she playing?

I contend that an overwhelming number of you would respond "yes" to each of the above questions. But the real answer is that we simply don't know because, for children who are developing physically, emotionally, mentally, and socially, the concept of play is as different as the kids are. Some children might consider being outside with their friends as play, while others might consider coloring a picture inside the home as play.

Regardless of these scenarios, play occupies a significant role in the development of all children, and it is clearly an innate biological need on the path to adapting to society. If you want to understand the importance of play, just look at other animals and notice the role it has in their development.

They run, they roll around, and they jump in what clearly looks to us like play, but all the while, they are exercising their muscles, developing agility and coordination, and learning the importance of working together.

This is much the same for young children whom we see at the playground running, jumping, and climbing in groups or by themselves. Can you imagine a child growing up without this sort of experience? Of course not. As caring parents and educators, we see the importance of this human activity we call play and strongly encourage our children to participate for their healthy well-being. Simply put, play is essential for a healthy body and mind.

Today, most adults believe that if their children are involved in organized sports, then they must be at play. However, that may not be the case. With organized sports, we have simply taken play, put it into an organized form, and added factors like skill development and discipline. But in doing so, we have changed the fundamental nature of play: It is no longer simply play; now, it is competition.

So how does this idea of competition fit in this context, and how do we so often confuse it with play in the world of organized sports for children?

The Concept of Competition

Competition is a contest in which the participants seek the same objective. Competition in children's sports is having a contest between one team or individual and another. With competition come rules, regulations, scoreboards, standings, and championships. It can either be awesome or ugly, and therein lies the problem. When competition dominates all the positive factors that are a part of sports, then the original goals of play are eliminated for many children.

The question is, does competition by its very nature destroy play? The answer is, not if it is conducted by those who understand the true meaning of play. However, that meaning is often destroyed when adults lose sight of the fact that competition for children must first and foremost be enjoyable, challenging, and fun.

Dr. James Humphrey is the author of an impressive book entitled *Sports for Children—A Guide for Adults,* in which he enumerates the following guidelines:

- Very young children in general are not very competitive but become more so as they grow older.

- There is a wide variety in competition among children; that is, some are violently competitive, while others are mildly competitive, and still others are not competitive at all.

- Boys are more competitive than girls.

- Competition should be adjusted so that there is not a preponderant number of winners over losers.

We can see from these guidelines that competition is a double-edged sword. It can enhance play in some children and ruin it for others. It is obvious that we must study the concept further. It is also obvious, in my view, that most coaches, administrators, and parents have not considered its effects in any depth at all.

Can we actually play while we're competing? The answer is, absolutely, but only if we're also having fun.

Several years ago I met Gary Warner, a member of the staff of an organization called the Fellowship of Christian Athletes. Gary had written a book on the issue of competition, and nowhere have I heard or read a more in-depth description on the topic. Here are three of the most compelling things Gary had to say:

- We are competing, not playing, when it begins to hurt, when we must make sacrifices and commitments, when we worry about defeat rather than fun, and when pressure and stress take over.

- It's perfectly all right to choose either play or competition— as long as you know what you are choosing, and why.

- People who don't care about records choose to play. Those who chase the records choose competition.

Winning a competition is the ultimate emotional release for the participant. It is a wonderful feeling that strokes the ego and fills the winner with pride. I maintain that the lessons we must teach and instill in parents, administrators, coaches, and children is not *whether* we won, but *how* we won. It is critical that we show disdain and disapproval for acts of cheating, brutality, intimidation, fear, and violence. These are the demons that can destroy healthy competition.

One day, a father called me to ask my advice about his son playing T-ball. He said that, each day, after he had dropped the boy off at practice and returned to pick him up, the coach told him that his son had cried from the moment he left until he returned. The father said to me, "So what do you think I should do?"

I simply responded that, at this point in time, perhaps the lad should consider music, art, drama, or something else in which he might have expressed an interest. Obviously, sports wasn't his "thing" right now. For him, it wasn't play; it was competition, and he wasn't quite ready for that just yet.

I believe that competition, instilled with the values of fair play, sportsmanship, and ethics, can help build character traits in young people that will last a lifetime. These are the traits we admire in the people with whom we want to work, play, and spend quality time. People with a competitive spirit are usually the leaders in every aspect of our society. So competition can be a positive thing, but if adults do not keep it in perspective, they can make children miserable and drive them away from sports.

WHY KIDS QUIT

A major reason for many of today's young participants to quit sports altogether is that sports simply aren't any fun for them. It's why a staggering number of youngsters are exiting playing fields across the country, many before they even reach their teen-age years.

Dr. Thomas Tutko, a psychology professor at San Jose State University and author of several books on the subject, explains the behavior of some children this way: "If children go to practice, perform painful drills, and improve their skills, but have no fun, and if the coach constantly hammers at their mistakes, after awhile, they're going to think, 'Do I really want to be here?'

"Often, we give a conditional label to kids who finally decide they really *don't* want to do this. We call them quitters. So the children may not have fun, *and* they're also labeled as quitters, an immense insult. Basically what you're saying is that they're not worthwhile." And Dr. Tutko sums it up by saying, "I can only believe that kids quit because their needs are not being met. In fact, they are meant to feel miserable."

Alex Walks Away

Over the years, I have heard a lot of "what drove me to quit sports" stories from people from all walks of life. One of the most vivid occurred right next door in our neighborhood in Newark, Delaware. The child's name was Alex, and when he was about five years old his father, a friend of mine, would take him out into the backyard to play catch. Alex was a text-book example of a child blessed with natural athletic ability, especially with hand-eye coordination, and he immediately caught on to catching and throwing a baseball. I noticed how quickly and easily he acquired new skills. I can still recall his father bragging to me one afternoon about how Alex was going to grow up to be a major league pitcher.

However, Alex's love was football, not baseball. My sons, Alex, and other neighborhood children used to play pick-up games of touch football in an empty lot down the street, and every day, they'd come home and talk about what a great player Alex was, how he'd get the ball to them on any pattern they'd run.

At the age of twelve, Alex began playing organized football in a local league. During his first year, he was the team's first-string quarterback and the team's most valuable player. He worked hard at improving his skills and enjoyed the praise of parents, peers, friends, and coaches. Alex was one of those special youth sports success stories, a shining example of all the good youth sports can bring to a child's life.

But the following year that all changed.

During the summer after Alex's first season, his original coach moved out of state because of a job transfer. So "Mr. G.," one of the other fathers who had been an assistant, moved up to head coach. With his promotion came a change in team philosophy. He believed that a good football team was a tough football team, and the way you got tough was by persevering in the face of difficulty and fear.

We'd hear stories about Mr. G.'s screaming at the kids when they'd make a mistake, or making them run laps as punishment for missing a tackle. But whenever Alex would complain, his father would rationalize it by saying, "You'll just have to grin and bear it this season." Maybe this tough-guy treatment would turn Alex into an even better player, his father reasoned.

Before long, Alex's dad told me that the boy was beginning to lose his usual enthusiasm for going to games and practices. As the season progressed, Alex's attitude slowly got worse and worse, and when the coach sensed that his star quarterback wasn't performing up to snuff, the last reason the coach suspected was his macho approach or his own philosophy. He knew only one course of action. If the coach had yelled a little aggressively at mistakes before, now he would be all over Alex, berating him for every failure, attempting to instill discipline where enthusiasm had disappeared. He wasn't going to let a bad attitude destroy the promise of his star quarterback.

At home, Alex's dad couldn't help but let his son know that he was disappointed with the mediocre performances he had seen during his recent games. It would have been one thing if he were trying his best, he would explain to me, but he knew that his son could do better, that he wasn't giving it his all. Worst of all, Alex didn't even seem to care anymore. When his father would question him about certain aspects of his performance, he would just shrug his shoulders. How could he explain to his father what he must have barely understood himself, that the reason he had always performed so well was that he had loved to play? But under the leadership of his new coach, football was no longer play; it was a chore, and the fun had gone out of it.

I was in the stands one day during a game near the end of the season when Alex threw a beautiful spiral pass that went straight through the hands of one of his receivers and fell incomplete. The coach immediately called a time-out. He was furious that the receiver had looked to see if he was about to get hit rather than concentrate on catching the football. "You gotta be tough enough not to care about getting hit," he barked to the young receiver.

Then someone said something to him. He spun around to see who it was who had the nerve to interrupt him.

"What?" the coach demanded, screaming. It was Alex. "What did you say?"

"I said that we all make mistakes, coach."

"There's no excuse for looking away from the ball like that," yelled the coach. "That's not a mistake, that's being a coward."

Those would be the last so-called words of inspiration that Alex would ever receive from this coach. He took off his helmet, removed his jersey and shoulder pads, and handed them to the coach.

"What do you think you're doing?" the coach demanded.

Alex turned away and began to leave, but after a few steps, he stopped and turned back around. "Not being a coward," he said as he walked off the field toward his father, who had come down from the stands to see what the problem was. What a sad moment for both of them.

Saddest of all, no matter how hard my friend tried, he

could never convince Alex to participate in organized sports again. His promising athletic career had come to a screeching halt at the ripe old age of thirteen.

What the Kids Have to Say

In recent years, kids just like Alex have been dropping out of sports at alarming rates. According to the surveys I've read, there are three major reasons cited by the children themselves:

1. It isn't fun anymore;

2. There's too much pressure on winning; and

3. The coaches present negative attitudes.

The problem is not that children don't enjoy playing sports—most children enjoy sports immensely under the right conditions—but that too many of the adults involved in youth sports programs fail to focus on the goal of *children having fun*. The adults do not appreciate the children's point of view. Thus, children are too often forced to adhere to an adult ideal of serious competition instead of being allowed to enjoy the simple pleasures of childhood play.

One of the most comprehensive studies ever done on youth sports by the Youth Sports Institute at Michigan State University listened to some of the reasons why children dropped out of sports told in their own voices. They listed the top ten reasons for boys as follows:

1. I was no longer interested;

2. It was no longer fun;

3. The sport took too much time;

4. The coach played favorites;

5. The coach was a poor teacher;

6. I was tired of playing;

7. There was too much emphasis on winning;

8. I wanted to participate in other non-sport activities;

9. I needed more time to study;

10. There was too much pressure.

They listed the top ten reasons for girls as follows:

1. I was no longer interested;

2. It was no longer fun;

3. I needed more time to study;

4. There was too much pressure;

5. The coach was a poor teacher;

6. I wanted to participate in other non-sport activities;

7. The sport took too much time;

8. The coach played favorites;

9. I was tired of playing;

10. Games/practices were scheduled when I couldn't attend.

There are depressing similarities in both lists, and I believe they support the positions I have taken. I believe it is time to review our philosophy, make the games more fun, and return sports to the children. If we can't, I believe children will continue to quit in huge numbers.

Children and Burnout

Philadelphia Eagle football coach Dick Vermeil was near the top of his profession in the 1970s. Because he was the head coach of a professional football team, the entire city followed his exploits, the press quoted his words, and he and his assistants developed and executed game plans designed to put a win in their record. In his powerful position, he made millions of dollars and influenced the futures of many. Still, Vermeil walked away from it all—and didn't return to the sidelines for more than a decade. Why? He was "burned out." Then, a few years later, the great Bjorn Borg walked away from tennis in his prime. Why? He was also burned out, another casualty of the demands that come attached with being one of the world's premier players.

Burnout not only affects those at the professional level. It is another factor that has crept into youth sports. It applies to both coaches and athletes who simply have grown weary of the enormous stress and demands placed on them to perform at high levels. Consequently, despite their incredible athletic gifts, they elect to quit the sport and move on to other pursuits. Think of all the gymnasts, swimmers, and others in various sports whose desire to play fizzles during their teen-age years.

Yes, burnout is claiming its share of younger athletes, too. It's absurd to think that we've got children eight and nine years old who are being forced to make a long-term commitment to a specific sport.

Many children are playing multiple sports twelve months each year. Their weeks are crammed with practices and games, mixed in with all-star teams and traveling teams.

For some, breaks and vacations rarely enter into the picture. Soccer season overlaps baseball, and baseball overlaps football, and so on. The result is that we have reached the point of saturation, a vicious revolving door of never-ending seasons. Some children are enduring multiple practices on the same day and are being sometimes forced to choose one sport over the other when their various game schedules intersect. In the process, they sacrifice their free time, which, in another era, would have been spent on schoolwork or with friends. Is it any wonder so many burn out?

Some parents must shoulder some blame. They have

become more demanding, and there's the feeling that if the neighbor at the end of the street is sending his son to football camp for a week, then I should, too. If their daughter is on the travel softball squad, then maybe mine should be, as well. We've got parents roaming around, armed with travel budgets, assuming the role of professional manager for their children. And they've got resumes highlighting their child's athletic exploits ready to hand out to coaches at the next level.

Too much "play" can quickly drain the fun from a child's participation. Parents with the best of intentions are turning their children into miniature workaholics with overloaded schedules that leave the youngsters exhausted at the end of the day, burned out. Children can't even take a couple of months' hiatus from a sport for fear of falling behind peers and being excluded from the team the following season. Equally troubling, many youngsters are pigeonholed into one sport by the time they reach their teen-age years and don't have the opportunity to excel in a variety of sports. Consequently, they're missing out on the chance to experiment with other sports, to learn and develop a variety of skills, and to work other muscle groups.

When I was attending a national symposium on youth sports recently, I read a local newspaper article devoted to the serious business of youth sports. It told of a local hockey player, all of twelve years old, who started playing before he had reached his fourth birthday. The article mentioned that he trained 300 days a year, spent his summers at hockey camps, traveled more than 4,000 miles annually, and spent thousands of his parents' money on hockey equipment, travel expenses, and ice time rental. I couldn't help but wonder if he and thousands of others like him will burn out before they even enter high school.

In my experience, children who suffer sports burnout are likely candidates to develop a life-long avoidance of physical activity. Youngsters involved in individual sports such as gymnastics, swimming, and skating are especially susceptible, although there are a growing number of children in team sports who are being affected, as well.

The Pressure to Perform

It used to be that serious sports waited until high school, but that's hardly the case any longer. Children are being introduced to organized competition at very young ages—along with the pressure to perform. Most children are reasonable and accommodating, and they really want to please parents and coaches. But if unrealistic demands are being placed on the children, then only tragedy can result.

Eventually all this outside pressure is going to back the children into a corner, and they're going to experience frustration and depression. Subconsciously, of course, they're pleading for the adults to ease up on the pressure. Continually being expected to perform up to a ludicrous set of standards can also take a physical toll. Headaches, muscle aches, sleepless nights, digestive problems, and other physical discomforts can all significantly affect our children's well-being.

Children who are subjected to these types of emotional torture suddenly become terrified of making a mistake. They fear they'll face a tirade from their coach or unkind words from their parents. When the playing environment becomes drenched in negativity, it can cripple the productivity and growth of a youngster.

At a conference concerning children and pressure, a good friend of mine, psychologist Orv Owens, had some interesting points to make in this area: "I know a corporation that promotes people by how many mistakes they make. And you can see how that frees them: All of a sudden they're relaxed, which means they don't make very many mistakes. But the person making the most mistakes is normally the one who's doing the most. In basketball there are a lot of players who will never shoot because they're afraid they might miss. In football, there are quarterbacks who will take a sack before they throw the ball—because they're afraid they're going to be intercepted. Well, the problem with that, of course, is if you never shoot the basketball, you will never score a basket. In football, if you don't pass the ball, you won't make any completions either. To be a good quarterback, you have to take the chance of a few incomplete passes or interceptions.

"It's true in any sport," Owens goes on. "You have to try, and make mistakes, fail, look really bad sometimes. And the coach will say, 'That was a good try. I'm glad you threw that pass even though it was intercepted because you were doing the right thing at the right time.'"

Owens advises, "And coaches should not give the impression they think any less of their athletes just because they missed a shot because if the athletes believe that, they won't take any more shots. They might not even come out to lace their shoes up to even play tomorrow."

Far too many children are, in fact, choosing that route, believing that to salvage their self-esteem and gain some relief from the intense pressure of participation, the quick solution is simply to quit. So not only are we teaching kids to hate sports, we are also implying that the best way to handle future problems is simply to walk away. I know that's not the message we mean to send our kids, but when burnout sets in, that's often the message they hear.

Humiliation Is Also a Factor

A few years ago, I had a vivid reminder of just how strong and indelible an impact a negative youth sports experience can have on the human psyche. I had been invited to be a guest on a radio sports talk show in St. Louis. For an hour, in addition to fielding calls from listeners, the host and I discussed all the problems children face in sports. I've spent a big part of my life listening to people vent their anger and discuss their concerns about the world of youth sports, but every once in awhile, there's a story that comes along that catches me off guard. This was one of those times.

We were deep into the show. I had just finished answering

a question from a listener, and the host jumped in and said, "Folks, I'm going to tell you my own story." I noticed that there was a whole new intensity to the host's demeanor. He began his story by telling me and the audience that as a child, he was short for his age and had a chronic weight problem. "I was the kind of kid that sports could have been really good for," he said. "In the right situation I'm sure I could have developed the skills to be a decent player, but I never really got the chance."

I could tell he was dealing with disturbing memories buried deep inside. He said that his father had decided that sports was just the thing he needed to toughen him up and whip him into shape, so when the youngster had reached the ripe old age of nine, his dad started signing him up for every available youth league.

The tryouts were always humiliating for him. "I was this fat little kid to them," he explained. "The only thing the coaches saw was my size and weight." The humiliation continued during the season. He was either ignored by the coaches and players or ridiculed by them. As a result, he was never seriously encouraged to improve.

During the games, he sat on the bench most of the time. One day, he was put in by the coach with about ten minutes left. His team had gained a thirty-point lead over the opponents. Every time they got the ball, his teammates would give it to him, telling him to shoot the ball. It was humiliating and embarrassing. When he missed or the ball was blocked by the taller players, time and time again, his teammates would laugh in amusement. This became a ritual for the team for the rest of the season.

"I wasn't a part of the team," he concluded. "I was a source of entertainment." His teammates were cruel and brutal, and his coach, who should have been teaching sportsmanship, fair play, and fun, did not stop them. Instead, he drove this youngster away from the game.

For years, the boy's father forced him to continue trying out for various teams. He grew to hate sports so much that he eventually began hoping that he wouldn't be placed on a team. Because his father demanded it, he would endure the torture, go through the motions at practices, and tolerate the taunts from other players and coaches. He was fourteen years old before he finally got the courage, on the eve of another try-out, to stand up to his father and refuse to participate in any more sports.

"In short," he said, "participating in youth sports made a huge portion of my childhood a living hell. If I wasn't being ignored, ridiculed, or humiliated, I was lying awake at night dreading the horrors that awaited me at the next practice or the next game."

There wasn't a lot I could say following this heart-breaking story, but I was completely stunned by what he said next. "You know, I have never told anyone this before," he said. "But one of the reasons my wife and I have never had any children is that I was afraid that my kids might go through the humiliation, hurt, and embarrassment that I was forced to live through."

Here was a grown man still feeling the pain of wounds inflicted years ago. It was a dramatic reminder of the serious, life-long imprint a negative youth sports experience can have. Ironically, it's the kids who are in the most need of a positive influence who often end up suffering the most abuse.

If this gentleman's father had access to a program that could have helped prepare them both for the world of youth sports, things might have turned out differently. We'll talk about such a program in the next chapter.

SPORTS: LEGALIZED CHILD ABUSE?

In 1984, I attended a conference on youth sports in which a pediatrician delivered a speech claiming that youth sports was "the greatest form of legalized child abuse in America." Like many in the audience that day, I sat there stunned. My initial reaction was, how could he make such a statement about something that had the wonderful ability to positively influence a child's life? Still, after really thinking about his presentation, I came to realize that the doctor had a point—a very good one. In recent years, it has become even more obvious. Just take a moment and look around the next time you're at a youth sports event. The negative words and actions of many coaches on the field and parents in the stands are truly shocking. It's also alarming to note that a recent study by the Minnesota Amateur Sports Commission (MASC) points out that abuse is running rampant in our sports programs. The MASC study found that when children were participating in sports:

- 45.3 percent of the youngsters surveyed said they had been called names, yelled at, or insulted;

- 21 percent said they had been pressured to play with an injury;

- 17.5 percent said they had been hit, kicked, or slapped;

- 8.2 percent said they had been pressured to intentionally harm others;

- 8 percent said they had been called names with sexual connotations;

- 3.4 percent said they had been pressured into sex or sexual touching.

These are grim numbers that point out in glaring detail that child abuse in America today has reached epidemic proportions. Child abuse in sports is any action taken by an adult resulting in the direct or indirect physical and/or emotional harm of children. It can occur verbally, physically, emotionally, and/or sexually.

All forms of abuse are destructive and detrimental to a child's growth and development, but emotional abuse seems to be the most common form of abuse in youth sports. When an adult places unrealistic expectations on a child, such as winning every game, scoring the most points, or playing without making any errors, that is emotional abuse. While this type of abuse is often more subtle than the others, it is equally devastating. When emotional abuse is delivered during growth periods, the expectations and the standards may haunt the children for a lifetime. These are the ones who are going to be chronically unhappy with their lives, always unsatisfied and unfulfilled because they never did quite enough. Failure will dominate their existence and devastate their spirits.

One of the most striking stories of emotional abuse was told to me during a 1985 conference on recreation I attended in Texas. After my presentation, a woman approached me and said, "I hope you realize how important your work is. I can't believe some of the things that we let happen to children playing sports," and she related the story of her son.

Brian, her eleven-year-old, had told her one day that all of his friends were trying out for baseball, and that he really wanted to make it into the league. Brian's experience playing baseball up until this point had been limited to pick-up games around the neighborhood. But for several weeks before the tryouts he worked hard every day with his father trying to improve his catching, throwing, and batting skills.

On the day of his tryouts, his hard work paid off, and he made the cut. He was ecstatic when the coach called him on the telephone with the news that he had made the team. For the next several weeks, his mother told me, Brian lived and breathed baseball.

Because of his relative inexperience playing baseball, Brian, like a lot of the other kids on his team, had been deemed second string by the coaches. On Brian's team, this meant that he was often neglected while the coach devoted time to working with the more experienced players who would help the team win their games. But in spite of this, Brian's enthusiasm never wavered. He showed up at every practice and gave his all without complaining. And though by the middle of the season he still had not been allowed to play in a single game, his mother said they encouraged him to persevere, instilling the value that just trying your hardest and doing your best was the ultimate goal in sports.

However, eventually, Brian began to wonder what the use was of going to practice every day and giving his all when it looked like the entire season was going to pass without his having at least one chance to put his hard work to use.

"Why won't the coach give me a chance?" he would ask his mother. But she had no answers for him. She didn't understand how a coach would have children work so hard and then never give them a chance to play. Then one day, she decided to approach the coach in private and ask him why so many of his players never got into the game.

"It wouldn't be fair to the other kids," he explained. "They work hard to be on a winning team. When they're out on the field, it's their job to do what it takes to win, and that's my job too. If I didn't play the best players, we'd lose, and that would upset everybody. Kids want to play on a winning team."

"Do you know what it says on the brochure they use to recruit all these kids to come out for this league?" she asked him. "It says, 'Youth Baseball, Don't Miss Out on All the Fun!' Do you think that it's fair to recruit kids in the name of fun and then never let them play? To make them work hard in practice after practice and then never let them put their hard work to use. Does that sound like fun?"

"I'll see what I can do," the coach told her. "But you have to understand that winning is what's fun."

"It's not fun to win if you didn't get a chance to participate in winning," she said to him. "Don't you think it's more important that these kids do their best and learn to accept whatever outcome comes from that? Or is winning all that matters? Do you realize my child is just eleven years old?"

The coach had no response. He was probably like a lot of coaches who want to keep things simple. If it's all about winning, they know exactly what to do; they feel competent, like an expert. But if it's about providing a good, positive, nurturing experience for kids, it all becomes very complicated. They ask themselves, "What am I supposed to be, a child psychiatrist?"

Then they go back to the old, familiar, easy course of attempting to guide their team toward winning and pretending that winning is the only thing that kids need or want. In fact, many coaches tell me that kids are happy just to be part of a winning team even if it means sitting on the bench. That may be true of a few, but one research study said that 78 percent of the children interviewed said they would rather play for a losing team than sit on the bench for a winning team. Brian was obviously one of those 78 percent.

After a short silence, the coach looked at Brian's mother. "I'll see what I can do," he repeated.

About a week went by, and then one afternoon, Brian burst into the house after a practice. He was beaming with excitement. "Coach says I'm going to play in Saturday's game," he proudly informed his parents. The day that he had worked so hard for had finally come. The mother secretly smiled to herself as she happily congratulated her son, feeling as if the talk she had given to the coach must have done some little bit of good.

When Saturday rolled around Brian's parents and grandparents were in the stands to watch Brian finally get a chance to play. They didn't expect to see him in the starting line-up or even to play during the first couple of innings, but they were anxious for him to be put into the game. By the fifth inning, since the game was tied, it was pretty apparent that he wasn't going to get a chance to play. By the last inning, they could see the hurt and embarrassed look etched across his face as he huddled by himself in the corner of the dugout, silent.

After the game Brian's mom confronted the coach, who explained that he had been expecting an easy victory that day since their opponents had one of the worst records in the league. But because the score was tight the entire game, he didn't think it would be fair to the team to risk losing the game by having Brian on the field.

While his mom spoke to the coach, Brian walked straight to the car and didn't say a word to anyone.

"The ride home was the toughest," she said. "There was nothing we could say to pick up his spirits. He simply sat there with tears in his eyes."

When they got home he went up to his bedroom and shut the door. He barely ate anything over the next couple of days and wasn't talking to anyone. Eventually, his parents had to enlist the help of a psychiatrist to help him deal with the impact of this experience.

"Baseball was Brian's first endeavor in the real world," his mother told me. She had brought him up to believe that if you worked hard and tried your best, you would get the chance to realize your dreams. And then one coach's thoughtlessness completely destroyed his world. Who knows what type of psychological scars he'll carry around with him during his adult years because of this one incident?

Brian's story is one that I'm reminded of over and over as I hear from people all over the country talking about their child's experiences in sports. If children are telling us that they have been called names, insulted, abused, and pressured to play with injuries, and they decide to drop out at an age when they most need sports in their lives, are we not developing children who are going to be that much more likely to resort to negative behaviors as a means of coping? If children are treated by their parents or coaches as worthless because they're not outstanding athletes, or because they dropped the ball, does this emotional pressure help encourage them to resort to unhealthy behaviors that may even include drugs, tobacco, and alcohol? Think about it.

PUTTING KIDS IN HARM'S WAY

The number of sports-related injuries sustained by children has risen dramatically over the past ten years. This increase can be attributed to a number of factors. One of the leading contributors is that more and more children are participating at a younger age; thus, as more children step on the field or the court, there are more opportunities for injuries to occur. In addition, there are other reasons for an increase in the number and severity of injuries: Youth sports seasons today are much longer than they were just a decade ago, there are more practices and games, and there is increased pressure to extend oneself in order to win one more for the team.

Injuries Are a Serious Concern

According to figures released by the U.S. Consumer Product Safety Commission, more than 775,000 children ages five to fourteen are treated in hospital emergency rooms for sports-related injuries each year. That figure doesn't even include all the children who end up seeking treatment at sports clinics or doctor's offices. Educated estimates of the total number of injuries begin at more than 5 million every year.

The long-term ramifications of childhood injuries are severe. One injury can have a domino effect on a child's still-developing body, setting off a grim chain of discomfort and pain. For example, an ankle injury that never completely heals before the child returns to play can lead to knee and joint problems later in life. We know well the ghoulish tales of professional athletes, particularly football players, who once sacrificed their bodies for fame and fortune and now hobble, limp, and maneuver around on a cane.

I believe it is ridiculous that children are paying this very steep price as well for a piece of short-lived glory. They may have helped the team win the championship or earned a shiny MVP trophy for themselves, but if it means not being able to play catch twenty years from now with their own kids, or not being able to bend over pain-free and scoop them up for a hug, it obviously isn't worth it.

All of the adults in charge must accept a share of the burden for many of these injuries. Volunteer coaches who haven't had any type of formal training are more likely to teach improper techniques; fail to conduct proper warm-up, cool down, and stretching exercises; neglect to provide relevant instruction in important areas of the sport; and send children into the games without all the necessary safety equipment. Parents are often guilty of returning injured children to the game without medical clearance, or encouraging their youngsters to "tough it out" and "be a man," putting their children in harm's way.

On occasion, we are caught up short when we hear a tragic story, and we suddenly realize how truly dangerous adult behavior can be. Such a tragic tale was told by Jane Wojick.

The Wojick Tragedy

I met Jane Wojick when I was asked by the ABC television news show *20/20* to be interviewed about issues involving safety in youth sports. They were doing a report on the heartbreaking story of what had happened to her son Ryan, who had begun playing baseball when he was in the first grade. While his parents never expected him to become a star athlete, they knew he loved to play, and encouraged his love of baseball, taking him to the park for sign-ups every year in the early spring. At the age of ten, he played the position of catcher for the Cardinals, his Little League team in Citrus Park, Florida. He weighed sixty-three pounds at the time, and stood about four and a half feet tall—a classic late maturer.

His mother enjoyed attending Ryan's games with her husband, but one day, because of a family commitment, she was going to miss most of his game. Late that afternoon, she arrived with her daughters at the ballpark and immediately noticed that the players were not out on the field. As she approached the bleachers, she overhead rumblings about someone being injured. Naturally, her first thought was of her son.

"Has Ryan been hurt?" From the sympathetic looks on the faces of the other parents as she approached, she knew that he had been injured.

A few minutes earlier, Ryan had been standing in the batter's box at home plate. With his team trailing, they really needed a hit. Ryan was up against a pitcher with an outstanding fastball who, like most ten-year-olds, hadn't yet developed the coordination to consistently keep his pitches under control. The hurler let loose a fastball that went high and inside, heading straight for Ryan.

He had tried to get out of its way, but there was no time. The ball struck him in the left side of his chest, just above the heart. Witnesses said he seemed to gasp for breath and then collapsed, unconscious.

His father rushed out of the stands and onto the field, desperate to help in some way, but Ryan lay motionless, his pupils fixed and dilated. He had no pulse. There was no sign of respiration. He was rushed to the hospital by helicopter but pronounced dead upon arrival.

There are many who see a case such as Ryan's as just another of the freak accidents that can and do happen anywhere, from riding a bike to climbing a tree. They claim these dangers are sad but inevitable. If kids are going to be kids, it is said, there are going to be dangers involved, and parents can't protect them completely.

Nevertheless, I would argue that youth league sports are activities designed and run by adults. Clearly, they should strive for a higher standard in providing an environment that is healthy and safe. So the natural question is, why are nine-year-old athletes with developing and widely varying coordination skills and limited athletic abilities competing with a ball that routinely causes injuries and has the potential to even kill?

It's not because a different ball would take away the fun for children. Indeed, at this age, when children are just developing the physical maturity and coordination required to field a ball with consistency, there is no greater threat to the fun of playing baseball than the fear of being injured by the ball. No, the reason why children are playing with hard balls is the same reason that causes so many of the other problems in youth sports. It is the sickness that the pediatrician diagnosed as "legalized child abuse."

If a softer version of the hard ball existed, would you not use it? Would it not improve the safety of the game? Would it not reduce the fear of injury? Well, as a matter of fact, such a ball does exist, and we'll discuss the use of the Incrediball in the next chapter.

In this section, we've focused on safety as it pertains to the child's point of view and baseball, but be assured the problem affects all sports. For example, Dr. Barry Maron of the Minneapolis Heart Institute reported that he has documented twelve cases, over the past fifteen years, in which young male hockey players died suddenly on the ice after being struck by pucks—or fists. In soccer, children who have only partially-developed neck muscles are taught to "head" a ball that is designed for much older children and adults; these constant blows to the head could create long-term effects. We could cite similar problems with field hockey, lacrosse, football, and others.

Many adults refuse to put the children's health and safety at the center of their focus when they design youth sports programs. Instead, they force children to conform to their own needs and desires to see an approximation of a professional sports experience. They want to see "little superstars" acting in accordance with their own yearnings—without regard for the children's well-being.

MANY SIMPLY AREN'T READY

A few years back the National Youth Sports Coaches Association commissioned a study of five- to eight-year-old athletes in the Cincinnati, Ohio area to see if they had the skills needed to successfully participate in their chosen sport. The children who participated in the survey were only asked to perform the most fundamental tasks of their sport like catching, hitting, and throwing in baseball, or kicking and running in soccer. The idea was to see if the kids could perform at a level that would allow them to participate successfully in the sport they had chosen. Of the 1,100 children in the survey, an eye-popping 49 percent were found to lack the minimum required skill level to successfully participate in their sport.

"Children who haven't been taught the fundamental skills and techniques of a sport before being placed in a competitive environment aren't going to have much fun participating," said Dr. Michael Gray, an exercise physiologist and director of Northern Kentucky University's Youth Sports Research Center, which conducted the study. "And they're not going to stay involved in the sport for very long either."

Over the years, I have seen the problems that can develop when a gap exists between a child's skill level and the requirements of their sport. The idea behind many of the athletic programs at the earliest levels is to provide a setting where children can learn the skills they will need when they move on to a more advanced level of the sport. Some parents enroll their kids in these programs to make sure their offspring will have an advantage when the leagues begin for the "real" sport. Children, anxious to please their parents, put on their team uniforms and go through the motions of real competition, but in too many cases, the young children haven't developed the athletic skills, physical strength, or motor coordination that their sport demands. The result is that their games are often more frustrating than fun. In our rush to envision our children as successful athletic competitors, we sometimes forget just how limited they are.

I have often tried to make this point by asking parents to imagine their child's second grade teacher as she walks into the classroom. She spends a few minutes going over the basic reading and vocabulary lessons that eight-year-olds typically struggle to comprehend, and then she says, "Enough of that," and begins distributing a big, thick book to her pupils.

"Today we are going to start reading a wonderful book called *War and Peace* by Tolstoy," she says.

Most parents don't have any trouble understanding that such an approach to reading instruction would be ridiculous, at best. The result would be boredom and frustration, because the language and the ideas would be far above the children's heads. The only "lesson" the students would learn is that they hate reading.

The problem for a lot of parents is that they are so hungry to see their children as successful athletes that they urge their kids toward *War and Peace*, while what they really need is a lot more time with *The Cat in the Hat* or *Winnie the Pooh*. If children responded exclusively to the desires of their parents, many would be serious competitive athletes at very early ages. Fortunately, they don't; they protest; they also have their own hopes and ambitions to pursue.

We can try to guide them with our love and praise toward facing their challenges on their way toward achieving their full potential in sports and every other aspect of life, but we must accept them with whatever their limited, individual abilities may be in these critical developing years. The key to that is seeing life, sports included, from their perspective, and respecting their point of view.

CONCLUSION

Children who are enrolled in youth sports are there, not because they are early maturers and gifted athletes, but because they are simply typical kids who are looking to have a fun time with their friends. One of the truly paradoxical situations involving children in organized sports is that while we speak in generalities that all children are alike, they are indeed very different emotionally, socially, mentally, and physically.

For this reason, I am continually asked, when do we treat our child as a competitive athlete and give her or him the encouragement and opportunity to reach maximum potential? My response is that, in general, some children will make the internal decision that competitive team sports are for them at about an age ranging from ten to twelve. This commitment may be a conscious decision or not; some children may not even know they have made a decision, but their attitude and behavior will change, nevertheless. They will begin to develop a love for sports out of the constant flow of praise from their parents, peers, and coaches, who find positive, genuine things to say: "What a great game you played today," "You've improved so much," "Wow, did you ever hit that ball," or "You're one of the best players on the team." The accolades go on and on, and with each one, the children grow in confidence and motivation.

This is a truly wonderful time in the lives of the youthful athletes. It is also the time when sports begin, and the idea of *play* is allowed to become *competition*, with a call for dedication, training, abiding by rules, and all the other commitments they must make in order to become the best they can be.

This is always a challenging period for the parents of the child. Now comes the task of helping to nurture this talent, helping it to grow and mature rather than wilt.

To sum up, children who are participating in organized sports don't deserve to be treated as miniature adults, to be pushed into competitive sports before they're ready, to be physically and emotionally abused, to suffer needless injuries, and to be pressured into sacrificing their childhood years for the sake of athletic excellence. It takes a lot of work to restore our youngsters' faith in working hard toward a goal when they are faced with negative experiences. Early adolescence is a time when children are looking for basic values that they can count on in their lives. Under the *right* conditions, many youth sports experiences can be enormously beneficial, teaching the importance of teamwork, cooperation, and hard work. In spite of this potential for good, many youth sports experiences, under the *wrong* conditions, can be emotionally damaging—and that damage can last a lifetime.

Thankfully, there are plenty of solutions readily available—these will be explored in the next chapter—that can be implemented to help ensure that all children have fun and rewarding experiences. After all, that's what youth sports are all about.

CHAPTER SEVEN

Solutions

If you have read the previous chapters, I hope that you have come to the conclusion that, while we have much to be thankful for in youth sports—concerned parents, dedicated coaches, effective administrators, and wonderful children—we nevertheless need to make some changes in the ways we conduct youth athletics in America. Those changes are the primary focus of this chapter.

Thankfully, a good number of solutions are readily available. Changing the way organized sports operate in America may not be as difficult as one might expect. Let me explain.

In my travels across the country, I have witnessed some remarkable things that coaches, parents, and administrators have done to help children enjoy their sports participation to the fullest. In addition to these first-hand experiences, I have attended countless conferences devoted to youth sports at which a number of individuals have shared with me successful programs they've operated in their own communities. The Alliance organization has also been instrumental in developing and implementing a variety of successful strategies of its own.

All of the suggestions offered in the following pages have had positive results in communities all across the country. They can make a positive difference in your community, as well. Solutions are at hand, if only we have the will to use them.

In the rest of this chapter, we will look at each of the problem areas we have examined, and explore practical solutions that can be adopted at the local level.

PARENTS

When we looked at the problems with parents in Chapter 3, it was evident that without the proper direction or a set of guidelines, many parents "support" their child's team with the mindset that they're watching the Super Bowl. We need to correct that. To do so, I recommend a two-pronged approach. First, set up a preseason meeting with all of the parents, and second, develop some strategies to keep parents on track once they understand what is expected of them. Let's examine each one in turn.

Institute an Orientation Program

When you start a new job, you go through an orientation program. When you enroll in college, you go through an orientation program. Taking the cue from those areas and having seen all the negative parental behaviors at games, our staff at the Alliance recommended that community youth leagues develop an orientation presentation specifically designed for parents. It would have two major purposes. First, we wanted to let the parents know they do play an important role in youth sports. Second, we want to define that role for and with them. The result was the Parents Association for Youth Sports (PAYS), which outlines what all parents need to know regarding their child and sports. With this parent orientation program in place, the potential for problems to arise during the season is greatly reduced.

This is a great idea, you say, but many parents won't attend, and most typically, they are exactly the ones who *should* be there. Well, in my experience, the most effective way to implement a parent program is to make it *mandatory*. If the parents can't set aside the half hour it takes to go through the program, their child doesn't get to play. Now this may seem a bit harsh, but it really is that important. Does it work? Absolutely. I've never heard of a single instance where parents have refused to participate when it would end up penalizing their child in the process.

The purpose of such a mandatory meeting is for the children's coach to sit down with the parents and spell out the philosophy of the league, explain what is going to happen to their children in the sport, and look at the role of the parents in the program. This is a chance for parents to get a clear understanding of areas such as practicing sportsmanship, supporting the child's performance, knowing the effects of an adult's negative behavior, having unrealistic expectations for the child, and handling sports injuries, among others. The coach will also take the time to answer the parents' questions and clarify any issues that might be raised.

It is most important that the child's coach conducts the meeting so that, from the very beginning of the child's sports season, the coach and parents have a clear communication link established to help overcome any misunderstandings. This way, both will end up pulling in the same direction in the best interests of the child.

This program outlines both the parents' rights and their responsibilities. For example, parents have the *right* to a safe and fun experience for their child; to have accurate and comprehensive information about the program; to be part of a quality program; to know about the procedure in case they have a complaint about a coach, a child, or an adult; and to be protected from retaliation if such a complaint is filed.

With those rights come *responsibilities*. Parents pledge to be good spectators; to assess the philosophy of the coach and league to make sure it matches their child's needs; to provide each child with physical nurturing, emotional support, and mature guidance; to understand that all children are gifted but not in equal ways; to provide unconditional love that's not based on performance; to create a safe and fun environment; and to pay attention to see if their child is having fun, learning, and improving—as opposed to just winning.

To Help Parents Stay on Track

Once parents have attended their orientation program and understand their role in the youth sports picture, we cannot assume they will maintain their decorum for the entire season. Oh, they may have signed the pledge with the best of intentions, but somehow, in some game situation, they may "lose it" and start some irrational behavior. What kinds of things can we do to help them to stay on track and maintain their "best behavior" in support of their children?

We never want to see fans banned from our youth games; that's a last resort. Parents play such an integral role in the whole youth sports process, and it's unfortunate to note that some youth leagues have had to resort to a parent ban at games. Under dire circumstances, that may be the most effective strategy, but it's my hope that leagues can introduce other measures that don't eliminate parents from the picture.

For instance, in Ontario, California there are approximately 600 boys and girls, ages five to fourteen, who participate in their local basketball program. Senior recreation supervisor Julie Dorey designed an innovative approach that has pushed the focus away from wins and losses for both the participants and the parents. The league doesn't keep standings, hand out first-place trophies, or even use the scoreboard during games, although the score is kept by someone on the sidelines. Supervisor Dorey and her colleagues are doing their best to promote children's play, eliminate "the scoreboard mentality," and keep the focus on sportsmanship and fun.

Dorey and her staff designed a sportsmanship rating program, where the behaviors of the coaches, parents, and children are rated on a scale of one to three. "The kids really pay attention to the sportsmanship award, and at the end of the

The Parents' Code of Ethics

These days, many youth organizations require that parents attend a comprehensive orientation program so the parents will understand the many aspects of their youngsters' participation. Others have gone a step further and require that all the parents of the children participating in the program sign the NYSCA Parents' Code of Ethics, pledging their cooperation as follows:

- I will encourage good sportsmanship by demonstrating positive support for all players, coaches, and officials at every game, practice, or other youth sports event.

- I will place the emotional and physical well-being of my child ahead of a personal desire to win.

- I will insist that my child play in a safe and healthy environment.

- I will support coaches and officials working with my child, in order to encourage a positive and enjoyable experience for all.

- I will demand a sports environment for my child that is free of drugs, tobacco, and alcohol, and will refrain from their use at all youth sports events.

- I will remember that the game is for youth—not for adults.

- I will do my very best to make youth sports fun for my child.

- I will ask my child to treat other players, coaches, fans, and officials with respect, regardless of race, sex, creed, or ability.

- I promise to help my child enjoy the youth sports experience by doing whatever I can, such as being a respectful fan, assisting with coaching, or providing transportation.

- I will require that my child's coach be trained in the responsibilities of being a youth sports coach, and that the coach upholds the Coaches' Code of Ethics.

- I will read the NYSCA National Standards For Youth Sports and do what I can to help all youth sports organizations implement and enforce them.

The Parents' Code of Ethics serves as a handy reminder of the type of behavior that is expected of the parents at all times.

It is used, for example, in the mandatory orientation program in LaPalma, California. Before the season begins, a special clinic is held that includes all the coaches, parents, and kids. The program covers everything from executing fun skills drills, to introducing the coaches, to explaining what type of behavior is expected from the parents. "It gets us off to a good start with the kids and parents," said Don Fromknecht, community services supervisor for the LaPalma Recreation and Community Services League. "We've heard a lot of positive comments."

If every league instituted a policy stating that no child could participate unless the parents went through such a mandatory orientation program, I believe many of the problems with parents would be eliminated.

season, it's the best award to get," Dorey said. In addition, the league uses "fan patrols" to monitor the behavior of the parents in the stands. Those who exhibit inappropriate behavior can cost their team valuable points.

I can already hear the traditionalists out there who are

saying, "Give me a break. This isn't sports. Sports are about winning, championships, and trophies."

And Dorey's response to that is, "I used to think that way too, but I changed my attitude after seeing the pain kids went through with this 'pro sports' mentality. I'd see parents yelling at their kids for not scoring or hustling. Everything was focused on the results on the scoreboard. Believe me, once we took down the scoreboards and kept score at the sidelines it made a dramatic difference."

While it is a sad commentary on children's sports, some leagues have instituted policies whereby any parent involved in a confrontation is given one warning to stop, either by the umpire or some other delegated sports official. If the behavior continues, those involved are asked to leave. If the individual refuses to leave, or leaves and then returns, the police are called. Based on the circumstances, the police may also charge the individual with criminal trespass. There's even a league in Georgia that pays for two uniformed police officers to be on hand during all games because the problems with parents have been so prevalent. I think it's sad that parents, who are supposed to be role models, act in a way that requires police action.

The bottom line is this: The best way to improve sports for kids is to *mandate* that all parents go through a pre-season orientation program. That's a more positive approach for dealing with parent problems.

COACHES

Next to the parents, the people closest to the children in sports are their coaches. You may recall that we explored some of the problems with coaches in Chapter 4. In attempting to deal with these problems, I present two major recommendations in this section. Let us insist, first, that our coaches be certified, and second, that they subscribe to a reasonable code of ethics. Let us explore both suggestions in a bit more detail.

Certification: The Road to NYSCA and Success

The battle to establish certification for coaches has proved to be long and difficult—and it's not over yet. To win the war, we must overcome two major obstacles. The first is the myth that "the way it's always been done is the best way." The second is that "we cannot make any demands on volunteers." I have become convinced that both beliefs are not only wrong but dangerous to the youth of America.

In 1980, after being totally frustrated with the attitude of coaches in youth sports, I took a leap of faith, left a good-paying job, and put all my energies—and life's savings—into forming the National Youth Sports Coaches Association, or NYSCA. My goal was to develop a national program to train and certify coaches. After a rollercoaster year of minor triumphs and major disappointments, I was able to secure the necessary funding through the generous support of three people—the heads of Puma, MacGregor sports, and Spanjian sportswear—who shared my vision and made a commitment to endorse it. NYSCA has never looked back.

After all was said and done, it turned out that the usual assumption that volunteer coaches would not submit to training proved to be a myth. The reality is that coaches *do* want training, *do* want guidance, *do* want to make a positive impression on their team. Without a doubt, training is the answer to those needs, and the success of the NYSCA certification program for coaches is the proof of that.

These are not just my personal beliefs; they are supported by solid research. For instance, in 1991, the National Research and Development Center at Northern Kentucky University (NKU) conducted a study on certification. They compared volunteer coaches who had been trained and certified by NYSCA with those who had not received any training.

The report concluded that many recreation professionals worried needlessly about offering mandatory youth sport coach certification. Their concern that certification would cause "a decline in volunteerism appears to be invalid." The authors found that both certified and uncertified coaches "strongly support" this training and would "rather coach for a league that required training." The uncertified coaches said a training requirement and payment of a fee "would not discourage them from volunteering to coach"; that they *would* voluntarily attend a certification clinic even if not required to do so; and that they would even "voluntarily seek out this training if provided the opportunity."

It seems clear that coaches are ready for change. They just need advice and direction on what to do in their community, which is exactly what our certification programs provide.

The Certification Process

Just what is involved with certification? Currently, there are approximately 2,200 NYSCA chapters in existence across the country, and only instructors certified by NYSCA conduct the actual programs. The training materials are on videotape, and the entire program can be taught in one evening. After viewing the video and discussing the concepts, the volunteer coaches take a short test to insure that they understand everything that was presented.

What does the "curriculum" look like? Well, being a NYSCA-certified coach does not indicate that the individuals are qualified to the same degree as paid coaches on the high school, college, or professional level. But as a result of their training/certification program, NYSCA certifies that they have been trained in the following responsibilities to children in sports: The coach will be aware of the psychological and emotional needs of the children participating; will understand that safety and first-aid care are the most important factors in the well-being of children; will know that only a person of medical authority (physician, paramedic, etc.) should be called upon to treat any kind of injury; will be aware of the importance of conditioning, nutrition, flexibility, and strength development; will be responsible for teaching proper sports techniques, to the best of his or her ability; will uphold the NYSCA Coaches' Code of Ethics Pledge, by which they are reminded that in youth sports, the consideration of the children should be placed above all else.

The NYSCA certification program is relatively inexpensive, and the cost of the program can easily be built into the registration fee for each child. Simply charging an extra dollar or two at registration will not keep families away from signing their child up. This small investment will help insure that children are playing for a certified coach who has received the appropriate training.

With training, coaches learn to understand the real purpose of youth sports: to provide *fun* for *everyone*. Training provides coaches with the opportunity to find innovative ways—such as the "Buddy Ball" program, discussed earlier—to include those who are mentally or physically disadvantaged. It also allows coaches to see the importance of providing girls with the opportunity to participate wherever and whenever they choose.

"My primary goal is to make sure that the kids have a good learning experience, develop skills for whatever sport they're playing, and have a positive, fun experience. This can only happen if the coaches are trained," said Bob King, an NYSCA volunteer in Tennessee. Bob is one of almost 6,000 recreation leaders who assists in conducting the program.

From our humble beginnings in the 1980s, when we certified only a handful of coaches, NYSCA has responded to the obvious need and now annually certifies more than 150,000 coaches in all 50 states. However, there are more than 2 *million* volunteer coaches in this country, and less than 20 percent have received any type of training from NYSCA or the handful of other programs that exist. While tremendous progress has been made, there is still much to do.

Certification Works

Is training effective? Absolutely. Since NYSCA's inception, more than 1.5 million coaches have gone through the program in the United States and around the world. The NYSCA program is not the only training/certification program that exists, but it is the nation's most widely used one, and the only organization that is governed by the actual membership of the coaches.

Does it work? Let me tell you a story that happened on a Saturday morning back in 1984. It might convince you that certification training is effective.

After watching the video presentation, one of the volunteer participants declared that he was "not fit to coach." One of the presenters on the video, Dr. Richard Magill, a sports psychologist, had made him confront what he had been doing as a coach for the past three years, and he had now decided that he had been "hurting kids."

As I looked at him, I felt a deep sense of pride knowing that our newly developed organization was on the right track. I assured him that he had just told me that the program works. If we can get people like him to look inside and see that children view every coach as their model, then we can really make a positive step in changing people's attitudes about coaching children in sports. If our training can do that, then we have accomplished our mission.

I urged him to continue coaching, telling him we need more good coaches with his kind of attitude.

My point is that our training program forces coaches to confront what they do with and the influence they have on youngsters. It helps them to change and grow. That's why NYSCA certification works, and why it's so important.

Research also supports that conclusion. As a follow-up to the study on certification mentioned earlier in this chapter, the Research and Development Center at NKU conducted a national study concerning the success of mandatory certification. They received responses from forty-five states which indicated that 93 percent of the communities reported a coaching certification mandate had made a positive difference, finding that trained coaches tended to be more cooperative, placed greater emphasis on fun and participation, and greatly improved the quality of instruction. Leagues, coaches, and parents all showed an increase in the acceptance of a mandate, once it was in place and operating. Mandated certification has arrived.

Helping to Keep the Coaches on Track

Simply because our coaches are certified doesn't guarantee that their behavior will always be 100 percent perfect. While inappropriate behavior is less likely to occur if a coach is certified, it still can happen. However, if there's a policy that works to police the behavior of NYSCA's coaches, the league administrators can remove those who don't live up to the standards of a volunteer coach. And because NYSCA is an organization governed by its own membership, the local league has the ability to implement such a policy without any red tape.

Every coach who goes through the NYSCA program is required to sign its Coaches' Code of Ethics, which emphasizes their responsibility to be positive role models. You can review these expectations by consulting the Inset on page 165.

If a complaint is brought against an NYSCA coach for violation of the Code of Ethics or any other matter, a local review committee is formed. This is comprised of three to five impartial individuals who understand the spirit and intent of the Ethics. The coach should also be invited to address the complaint and to offer his or her side of the story. The local review committee has the complete authority to determine the severity of the situation, whether the coach has violated the Ethics, and if the coach should be permitted to retain certification. If the local review committee has a majority vote to revoke certification, the coach does have the right to appeal to the National Executive Board.

Surely, our youth league coaches are not all that bad, you say. After all, they volunteer to work with children and have the youngsters' best interests in mind. I wish that were true,

Coaches' Code of Ethics

These days, many youth organizations require that coaches attend a comprehensive certification program so they will understand the physical, emotional, and social needs of youngsters; so they will keep fun, sportsmanship, and participation as their primary objectives; and so they know they are perceived as role models. Furthermore, coaches are required to sign the Coaches' Code of Ethics, pledging their cooperation as follows:

- I will place the emotional and physical well-being of my players ahead of a personal desire to win.

- I will treat each player as an individual, remembering the large range of emotional and physical development for the same age group.

- I will do my best to provide a safe playing situation for my players.

- I will promise to review and practice the basic first aid principles needed to treat injuries of my players.

- I will do my best to organize practices that are fun and challenging for all my players.

- I will lead by example in demonstrating fair play and sportsmanship to all my players.

- I will be knowledgeable in the rules of each sport that I coach and I will teach these rules to my players.

- I will use those coaching techniques appropriate for each of the skills that I teach.

- I will remember that I am a youth sports coach and that the game is for children and not adults.

This is the NYSCA code of ethics, but I firmly believe that every coach should be asked to subscribe to it, and act accordingly.

but, sadly, a number of NYSCA coaches have had to be disciplined. Here are a few examples of why such a drastic action has been necessary in the past:

- A baseball coach sent one of his players up to the plate *without* a bat, and told the umpire that this player never swung at a pitch and didn't need a bat. The opposing pitcher refused to pitch to the youngster, and the coach created such a scene that he had to be removed from the park before the game could continue.

- A soccer coach arrived late for practice forgetting he still had his derringer in a holster; he handed it to one of his nine-year-old players and asked him to place on the bench.

- A baseball coach for eleven- and twelve-year-olds put up his fists and informed the umpire he was ready to fight.

- A coach of a baseball team for eight-year-olds was caught showing one of his players pornographic magazines in his truck while practice was taking place. Upon further investigation, authorities found all sorts of pornographic materials in the coach's home, including more than 600 photos of children.

In each of these cases—and all too many others—youth league coaches have had their certification revoked. If coaches know they will be held to the Code of Ethics standards and may face disciplinary action, they are more likely to maintain high standards and act in the best interests of the children. And if they do not, despite the best training available, they should be disciplined. Now, because of NYSCA, we have a rationale and a procedure for action.

The first task, then, is to see that each coach on each team is certified to coach. Then, the league should keep the coaches on track with continued training and review, attention to the Code of Ethics, and disciplinary procedures, where necessary. If we do all of this, our children will be the beneficiaries.

OFFICIALS

Competent officiating is a necessary component of any youth sports program, but many times, leagues must recruit volunteer umpires, referees, and other officials to do the job. Nevertheless, the best alternative is for the league to employ certified officials. This seems obvious, given the importance of youth sports and the need for consistency, integrity, and professionalism in our officials. Through our National Youth Sports Officials Association (NYSOA), certified officials learn and develop basic skills, mechanics, and fundamentals, as well as understand how to have fun and enjoy the experience, despite the pressure and anxiety to perform to perfection.

Many programs that require their coaches to be certified are demanding that their officials also be certified. I believe that's a big step in the right direction. For example, the Plano Sports Authority (PSA) in Plano, Texas, requires all its volunteer coaches to be certified. The PSA was the first organization to require its officials to be certified by the NYSOA.

"We felt that because we are such a strong youth organization that the focus for our officials needed to be on the same skill level as our coaches," said Mary Margaret Taylor, executive director of the PSA. "And the NYSOA program trains officials in exactly that way. It's been surprising that even after the veteran officials watch the video, they're very pleased with what they've seen. They've been very surprised that there was any type of training for youth officials and that the tape covers things they didn't even think about."

The NYSOA certification program for officials is similar to the NYSCA program for coaches but takes just eighty minutes to complete. It includes information that every good official must possess. Officials who are certified through the program are also required to sign the Officials' Code of Ethics. This code—printed on page 169—should govern the officials on the court, in the gym, or on the field. Violation of the code can result in disciplinary action.

In addition to the NYSOA certification program, there are

other training programs that do an excellent job. One of the best is the Western Suffolk Baseball Umpires Association (WSBUA), on Long Island, New York. All prospective officials must attend five training sessions covering rules, mechanics, safety, sportsmanship, and problem-solving. After this, they are given a written examination and a field test. If they pass both, they are certified. To maintain that status, each year they must attend five meetings, at which rules, interpretations, mechanics, and other issues are reviewed. In addition, they must pass an annual certification examination. In 1995, WSBUA instituted annual mandatory workshops to improve mechanics, knowledge, and attitudes. These training seminars have two parts, a video/discussion session and a mechanics session. Any umpire who doesn't attend both is de-certified.

If the officials in your community don't have such training and certification programs, perhaps your league administrators should consider their adoption. The entire youth athletics program will benefit.

ADMINISTRATORS

If you recall Chapter 5, you know that the league administrator's role is crucial to the success of the program. In this section we will look at suggestions for improving their performance, as well as that of the local park and recreation directors. We will suggest that, where applicable, they control their fields by use of their permit authority; seek adherence to the National Standards for Youth Sports; seek training in the variety of aspects to their positions; promote the elimination of gender discrimination; and encourage inclusion of the disabled on their teams and in their programs.

Let's examine each of these recommendations more closely.

Recreation and Park Directors Must Take Charge

Almost every community of any size has a parks and recre-

Officials' Code of Ethics

Many youth leagues have recognized the importance of trained, consistent, competent officials, and have acted to require their sports officials to be certified, many under the auspices of NYSOA. As part of the certification process, the officials are required to sign this Officials' Code of Ethics:

- I will encourage good sportsmanship by demonstrating positive support of all players, coaches, fellow officials, and league administrators at all times;

- I will insure that I am knowledgeable of the rules of each sport I officiate at, and apply those rules fairly to all participants, teams, and coaches;

- I will not allow personal friendships and associations to influence my decisions during a contest;

- I will refrain from the use of alcohol and tobacco products when in a youth sports environment; and

- I will remember that youth sports is an opportunity for children to learn and have fun, and I will place their safety above all else.

   Because of the code, officials clearly know what is expected of them, and they know that violation of the code can result in disciplinary action by the league. Because of the code, I firmly believe our certified officials will act in a more professional manner, and our children will benefit.

ation department whose purpose is to provide area families with places for recreation. As I stated early on, over 60,000 athletic facilities have been built to accommodate the growing need for scheduled games. Look around your community. Somewhere, you'll find parks and recreation directors signing permits for the use of their youth sports facilities; also, school district superintendents will allow a variety of leagues to use their athletic facilities. It is with this "power of the permit" that we can take the important first step in the action plan to change the present day system.

Who's Running Youth Sports, Anyway?

I once attended a recreation conference where the speaker asked an interesting question of the directors of city recreation, the administrators who issue permits to volunteer organizations wishing to use "Northwest Park," a local ballfield. He said, "Are you running youth sports in your community or are they running you?" I wasn't surprised that almost every person in the room admitted that youth sports were running them. That seems to be the way it is across America. Why should that be so?

It seems that what we have done wrong over the years is to allow the tail of the volunteer administrators to wag the community dog. Why? It happens because the volunteers do all the work of raising the funds to operate a league, purchasing uniforms and equipment, buying insurance, and recruiting coaches—the list goes on and on. Running a youth sports organization of any size is often like a full-time operation.

All of this may be true, but just because volunteer parent groups do all the work does not mean that those parks and recreation directors and those school superintendents who lease the facilities should do so with just a rubber stamp, with no requirements or standards of behavior to follow. Yet that is exactly what most communities have allowed to happen over the years.

As a necessary first step in changing the system, community parks and recreation directors and school superintendents must institute a review and certification process. As part of that procedure, they might ask the following questions:

170

- Does the organization have a statement of purpose? Do they have bylaws, and are they followed?

- Who is eligible to participate in the program? How do we know such eligibility is strictly enforced?

- How are the funds used? How are they reported?

- Is there a method to screen volunteers for coaches? Officials? Are the coaches and officials certified?

- Does the league have liability and accident insurance? What provisions have been made for the safety of the participants?

- Does the organization have a disciplinary procedure governing its volunteers?

- Does the organization provide training for volunteers?

- Are they themselves trained in some phase of child development?

- Do they implement the National Standards for Youth Sports? (See page 173.)

Once the local recreation agency or school district has asked their questions and completed their assessment of the existing youth sports scene, it can then establish the criteria for any and all leagues wishing to use their community or school facilities.

Here is the key: *If a youth sports organization or league fails to meet the criteria, it should be denied a permit to use the community or school facilities!* This is the method by which local communities and school districts can assert their rights and take back control.

"National Standards" and Permits

As a guideline for communities, the Federal Office for Substance Abuse Prevention funded a national convention of experts in the field of youth sports. The discussion was designed to establish national standards that would provide families with a focus on what is best for their children in their younger years when they are still learning and growing. The resulting "National Standards for Youth Sports" have been endorsed by hundreds of recreation agencies across the nation and place in motion a national policy for children's sports.

Think of how much we could change the world of youth sports if communities and schools established the criteria that stated, "All volunteer youth sports leagues wishing to lease local community facilities must agree to adhere to the National Standards for Youth Sports." Of course, if they did not adhere to the National Standards, their permits would be revoked, and they would not be allowed to use the community or school facilities.

Communities must take back their sports and return them to children. The mechanism to do so rests with the field permits in the hands of our parks and recreation directors and our school superintendents. Permits are powerful weapons, and our local administrators should use them to bring about positive change. Let them exercise their administrative leadership.

Require League Administrators to Be Trained

We've discussed the importance of having trained coaches and officials; the same applies to administrators. A few years ago, our Alliance organization came to the realization that if we didn't do something to help administrators in their jobs, we weren't doing *our* jobs completely. With that in mind, we set out to create the Academy for Youth Sports Administrators, an eight-course program that provides professional and volunteer youth sports administrators with the training and knowledge to handle more effectively their various responsibilities.

National Standards for Youth Sports

When community organizations and schools allow leagues and teams to use their facilities, they grant them a permit to do so. Currently, most leagues or teams need only to apply and they receive the permit. What I have suggested is that the permission must *not* be automatic, that the league or the team requesting the permit must pledge to live up to the National Standards for Youth Sports. If they do not, they fail to get the permit and will not be able to function. Through this use of the "power of the permit," communities and schools will be able to control who uses their facilities and how they do so.

The National Standards were developed by experts in the field of youth sports at a conference sponsored by an arm of the federal government. As adopted at the local level, the National Guidelines might include the following:

- Teams must consider and carefully choose the proper sports environment for their children, including the appropriate age and development for participation, the type of sport, the rules of the sport, the age range of the participants, and the proper level of physical and emotional stress.

- Teams must select youth sports programs that are developed and organized to enhance the emotional, physical, social, and educational well-being of the children.

- Teams must encourage a drug-, tobacco-, and alcohol-free environment for their children.

- Teams must recognize that youth sports are only a part of a child's life.

- Leagues must insist that coaches are trained and certified.

- Parents must make a serious effort to take an active role in the youth sports experience of their child, providing positive support as a spectator, coach, league administrator, and/or caring parent.

- Parents must provide positive role models, exhibiting sportsmanlike behavior at games, during practices, and at home, while also giving positive reinforcement to their child and support to their child's coaches.

- Parents must demonstrate their commitment to their child's youth sports experience by annually signing the Parents' Code of Ethics Pledge.

- Leagues must insist on safe playing facilities, healthful playing situations, and, should the need arise, proper first-aid applications.

- Parents, coaches, and league administrators must provide equal play opportunity for all youth, regardless of race, creed, sex, economic status, or ability.

By insisting on the National Standards for Youth Sports, the local parks and recreation directors and school superintendents would accomplish two things. First, they would take back control of their facilities. Second, they would forge a partnership among parents, teams, and leagues in the best interests of children. Those would be some accomplishments.

The Academy features comprehensive courses on youth sports philosophy, planning, parental involvement, volunteers, child abuse prevention, financial management, risk management, leadership, and professional enhancement.

We believe it gives our administrators the tools, training, and confidence to run their local league operations in an effective, professional manner. Along with the classes, there's an opportunity for administrators to talk with one another and share ideas and solutions to common problems. The Academy programs typically take two days, and they are held at different sites around the country. We've even conducted one in Germany for youth sports administrators stationed overseas.

"Youth sports in my military community will benefit as a result of my attendance at the Academy for Youth Sports Administrators," said Ed Fuller, youth sports director for the United States Air Force at Aviano, Italy. This was echoed by Ross Hatchell, president of Parker Dixie Baseball in Florida, who said, "This was the best learning experience I've had so far. Every person involved in the administration of a youth sports program should be required to attend."

One of the best administrators I've met over the years is Bill Baggett. I've known Bill for a long time, and I am convinced he could manage a Fortune 500 company with no problem because that's how he managed the Juno Beach (Florida) Little League. He was among the first to see the need for administrative training and saw to it that his youth sports administrators took advantage of the Academy training. As a result, he had full confidence in his administrative people and was able to delegate skillfully to individuals who headed the committees that raised funds, ordered the equipment, created the master schedule, and more. Bill ran the league so that each youngster had a positive, safe experience. He also saw the need for every coach to be trained, and his became the first league in the state of Florida to mandate that no coach would be assigned a team unless the head coach had been certified by NYSCA. Other youth sports administrators would do well to follow the example of Bill Baggett.

We should require all volunteer administrators who take on the responsibility to run youth leagues to have basic training in the management of youth sports. It's a wonder that we have never made this a requirement from the beginning.

Girls and Sports

You may recall we discussed the importance of girls' playing sports in Chapter 5. Primarily, the responsibility for ending gender discrimination falls to the local youth league administrators. Certainly, coaches and parents have a role in this area, but it is the administrators who must set the tone. That's why whenever youth athletics programs are offered in a community, the league's by-laws and all of its promotional materials should clearly state that they are open to both boys and girls.

The principle is this: Girls should not be denied the right to participate in any sport, at any level. To deny them full participation amounts to gender discrimination.

Thus, it is up to the responsible administrator to recommend changes, rewrite policies, and suggest improvements to the league's board of directors. It's imperative that girls receive equal opportunities to participate, and it's vital that administrators work to eliminate gender discrimination. League actions must be in the best interests of all young participants—not just the boys.

Including Disabled Kids

As we said in Chapter 5, including children with disabilities in mainstream sports may seem like a foreign concept, but it shouldn't. Their inclusion can truly be a positive experience for everyone involved. While the parents and the coaches have a role, it is the league administrators who should take the lead. They must recognize that, while the most important influence is going to be on the child with the disability, an inclusive policy also plays a key role in helping the other kids—and adults—to recognize and appreciate the differences we all have. Also, it helps them understand that all individuals, regardless of their physical and emotional differences, can contribute in their own special way to the total youth sports experience.

Tom Schie's experience would be a good example. Tom, of Lawrenceville, Georgia, has done many wonderful things for his community, but it was one special thing that really stood out. A neighborhood youngster, Kyle Maynard, had been born with arms and legs that had stopped developing at the joints. Despite his disability—and his wheelchair—his dream had always been to play football with his peers. So when Kyle appeared at the league sign-up, Schie picked him for his team, and the league administrators, true to their inclusive philosophy, supported his decision. Somehow, they would make this work. The players quickly accepted Kyle as part of the squad, and he played nose tackle on defense. During the season, he averaged three tackles a game and even recovered a fumble during one game. Kyle was a youngster who had been confined to a wheelchair, but Schie was able to look beyond the physical disability to see a child who loved football and simply wanted a chance to play. He made it work, and Kyle will now have some truly wonderful memories to treasure for the rest of his life.

Including kids with disabilities in activities with their peers who do not have disabilities is a major guiding principle of the Americans with Disabilities Act, which we reviewed in Chapter 5. It also should be part of the philosophy and practice in the local community, as it is in Lawrenceville, Georgia.

Consider the philosophy of Cindy Burkhour, a recreation consultant, who has been working with kids and adults with disabilities for fifteen years. Through her efforts over that period, some wonderful ideas for helping to bring the disabled into mainstream sports have been implemented.

In basketball, for example, a child who has limited movement in the legs could be the designated free-throw shooter for the team. Whenever a player on that team is fouled, the designated free-throw shooter enters the game to attempt the free throws. It's a simple yet effective way to include the disabled child on the team.

Where do such ideas come from? All it takes is a little ingenuity on behalf of the league administrators and coaches to come up with some creative solutions. You may recall Beth Campbell, who developed a youth baseball program called "Buddy Ball," where disabled children participate right alongside able-bodied children. Ideas can come from anywhere. And don't forget the children themselves; they are a great source of ideas for how to include their friends, too.

Certainly, league administrators ought to take the lead in bringing Buddy Ball and other innovative programs to their community so that the disabled can know the benefits of sports, too. Do you remember the philosophy of Bill Hughes: "Everybody plays"? Well, that applies to the disabled youngsters, too, but it will only happen if league administrators exercise some leadership.

SAFETY: A HIGH PRIORITY

When it comes to the safety and health of our precious children, parents, coaches, and administrators each have a role. Parents have the primary responsibility to see to the health of their offspring, and must teach them from the earliest age to be careful of the many dangers that surround them. Parents also have a role when it comes to their youngsters' sports participation. They are the children's first teachers and playmates, and in those roles, they can promote safety and respect for others.

However, the major responsibility for safety on the court, on the field, or in the gym falls to the league administrators and their coaches. Administrators do not often come in direct contact with children, but they can have a strong influence on safety. For example, through their regulations, they can make sure parents will attend an orientation program, and that coaches and officials will be certified; through the power of the purse, they can make sure that safety equipment is purchased

178

and used; through their regulatory power, they can implement policies banning such dangerous practices as spearing in football or hockey, or dangerous slides in softball or baseball. Coaches must train the children to wear the proper equipment, get them to use the apparatus properly, and, like the parent, teach them to avoid reckless or dangerous behavior.

In addition, in the following sections, I offer some specific suggestions for creating the safest possible environment for the children.

Keep a Log

Logs are useful safety tools because they enable the coach to recall how specific situations were handled. For example, if coaches are involved in lawsuits that come to trial two or three years from now, such detailed logs will give them specificity and credibility. In the log, the coach should record practices, drills and, exercises; note any injuries that occur, including details like time, place, severity, and action taken. They should also indicate when the equipment was inspected; list any telephone calls to parents or other authorities regarding problem children, fans, officials, and the like.

Have Every Parent Sign a Consent Form

From a liability standpoint, there isn't much value in such a form because a parent can't sign away the child's right not to be treated negligently. However, it's still important because it shows the parent consented to the child's participation in the sport. On the consent form, there must be a statement that injuries are part of the game, that they're going to happen on occasion, and that the coach is not responsible for them. A medical authorization form should be included, allowing the coach to obtain emergency medical treatment for the athlete in case the parent isn't available. Administrators should think about a medical authorization form, filled out by the athlete's physician, attesting to the child's fitness to play and listing allergies, vision, and special problems. These forms should be handed out at a preseason meeting with parents, and children should not be permitted to participate unless the forms have been returned.

Inspect the Playing Area

It's important that the coaches and administrators inspect the playing area before every practice and game. If it's an outdoor facility, it's a must to check for rocks, holes in the ground, broken glass, or anything else that could harm a child. If it's an indoor facility, the surface should be checked for loose floorboards, wet spots or any dangerous condition. If any problems are found, they should be reported to the maintenance department. Whoever is inspecting should record observations and follow-up actions in the log.

Use the Safest Equipment Available

Countless injuries could be prevented by adopting a few innovative suggestions in our youth sports leagues. I've heard Jane Wojick speak so passionately—you can read some excerpts on pages 183 and 184—about the kinds of innovations that might literally save lives if they were adopted. These would include things like the following for baseball:

- Attach face shields to batting helmets to prevent facial and eye injuries;

- Use quick-release bases that give way on hard impact to help reduce sliding injuries;

- At first base, use two bases side by side, one in fair territory for the fielder and one in foul territory for the runner; this will help to cut down on the possibility of collision.

These kinds of things, and more, are available on the market today. Nevertheless, the stubborn baseball traditionalists,

An Incrediball Idea

You must know that the regulation baseball is hard, especially for youngsters just starting out. Often they are afraid to catch it, and when they do, it stings their hand, even with a glove on. Often, when they are fielding, they are afraid of being hit in the face, especially if they wear eyeglasses or braces.

Our Alliance organization suggests that leagues consider a softer, safer alternative for children who are being introduced to baseball or softball through programs like T-ball. Soft-textured balls, like the Incrediball, are softer than a regular baseball, and they have seams that bulge out a bit so a youngster's little hands can properly grip and throw it.

Imagine how many injuries might be avoided if every league mandated this kind of ball for children playing at the T-ball level. We're never going to eliminate injuries, but we can cut down on fear, teach basic skills, and build confidence.

many of whom are administrators and presidents of youth baseball programs across the country, turn their back on these suggestions. Their warped reasoning is that it's not how baseball was played when they were growing up, and it's not how baseball is played at the Major League level. That's a pretty disturbing attitude, considering what kinds of injuries we have been seeing in recent years. However, if administrators and coaches want the safest environment possible, they must keep an open mind and consider new approaches to keeping the game safe for the children.

Check the Equipment Regularly

It might be great that we have the latest, safest equipment, but if it's not used appropriately, or if it has defects, that may cause more harm than good. Before using the gear, the coach should make sure that it functions properly. During the season, the coach should continue to check for any defects. These inspections should be recorded in the log.

Make Sure One Adult Present Knows Emergency Care

When adults are assisting on the field, the administrators or the coaches should make sure there's always someone qualified in first aid and CPR. In fact, administrators should consider such training as a *requirement* in their coaches' certification program.

Plan for Injury

Just as the coaches plan for game situations during practice sessions, they should plan for an injury situation on the practice field, doing all the things that one would do if an actual injury occurred. The coaches should know whom to call and have the consent forms and the medical authorization forms at hand. Later, when the injured player wants to return, the coaches should make sure the child has a doctor's authorization.

Coaches and administrators who follow these guidelines, use common sense, and observe the code of ethics will go a long way toward helping insure that each child has a safe and positive sports experience.

Establishing a safe sports program for our youngsters is a team effort. It involves parents, coaches, and administrators working together, as we have discussed. Injuries will always be part of the game, but they should not happen because we failed to do our very best to prevent them. Safety must be a high priority for all involved. After all, these are children we are dealing with.

Jane Wojick's Speech from the Safety Summit

In Chapter 6, I mentioned Jane Wojick's poignant speech about her young son, Ryan, who died on the ballfield as the result of a wild pitch. Her speech to the Safety Summit had a strong effect on so many, but it also had concrete recommendations about safety. Here is a sampling:

Ryan began playing baseball in the first grade. He would play spring and fall, if we got him to the park in time to sign up for the league. We realized he would never make a living out of this, but he had a good time playing. That was the important thing.

One Saturday, Ryan was in the kitchen making nachos in the microwave, and I was explaining the day's schedule. Ryan turned to me and said, "Mom, today I'm going to steal two bases."

I looked at him and said, "Ryan, you don't have to steal two bases." Then, I pulled him toward me, saying, "Ryan, I love you," and gave him a big hug and a kiss.

He turned around and said, "I love you too, Mom."

Later, the girls and I arrived at the ballpark, only to find out that Ryan had been injured, hit by a pitch that got away. An hour later, he was pronounced dead at St. Joseph's Hospital in Tampa. . . .

Our son's death was completely preventable.

You have listened to all the presenters this weekend speak of just how fragile these youngsters are. These are children. They are not miniature adults—not miniature reproductions of ourselves—and they're not our second chance to live a dream that is forever gone.

With time and the evolution of sports, we have seen many changes. We have watched football evolve from simple shoulder pads and lightweight leather caps to full padding from head to toe. We have watched hockey do the same. In baseball, we may have improved the equipment, but we have never improved the safety. I did see new stands being built, and a new press box, but I never saw any changes for the child.

I'm not asking you to change the game; I'm asking you to protect the children. At this conference, we have seen the new balls, protective vests, breakaway bases, face guards, and all of the other things vendors have to offer. Why not offer balls that are softer? Why not chest protectors? Why not face guards? These items will increase the safety and the confidence of the children.

Because we don't take preventive measures, I will never again have the opportunity to hear Ryan say, "I love you too, Mom."

Every youth league administrator should remember Ryan Wojick and his family when ordering equipment, recommending by-laws, conducting orientation programs, and considering coaches' training.

CHILDREN

One of the greatest experiences parents will ever have is teaching their children to ride a bicycle. I should know, I helped all seven of my kids learn to ride. It's truly thrilling to take off a set of training wheels and proudly watch your child peddle safely down the street.

I've often wondered what it must have been like before training wheels appeared on the scene. How many children were there with scraped knees, bloody elbows, and bruised butts before some genius came along and said it doesn't have to be this way? Think about it: Training wheels allow children to learn how to ride the two-wheeled devil without the fear of crashing; they instill confidence in the youngsters' abilities to maneuver in any direction without accident. The entire experience is typically a positive one and probably makes for a fond childhood memory.

So how come in sports, the same "training wheels" philosophy is typically ignored? We don't throw calculus, *War and Peace,* or the Periodic Table of Elements at our youngsters—until they're ready. But in a sport like baseball, we give them oversized baseball gloves and force them to play with a hard baseball. Or we expect them to dribble regulation-sized basketballs and shoot at standard ten-foot baskets.

Let me make this recommendation: Before the parents ever sign their children up for an organized sport, and before those children ever set foot on a playing field, the youngsters must go through some type of pre-sports readiness program, a sort of training wheels for sports. A few years ago, such a program was simply a concept. Today, it has grown into a proven way of introducing sports to all kids. There are obviously a number of approaches to insure that children are ready for organized sports, but let me explore one unique idea that has been extremely successful.

Starting Smart, a Training Wheels Program

I was fortunate enough to be a part of Start Smart from the beginning, and I have taken great pleasure in watching how it has influenced the lives of so many children. Let me explain.

Back in 1992, I received a telephone call from Barry Golombik, who was a key person at the company that makes the Koosh Ball, those colorful, soft products that kids love to throw around in the yard. Barry suggested that we work together to develop a series of products that would help children learn how to catch, throw, and hit, yet still be safe, fun, and challenging to use. I thought this was a great idea, but suggested we take it a step further: If we worked through the parents, they could understand how to use these products with their children, and know firsthand what benefits could be derived from learning and developing these skills.

That telephone conversation was the impetus for the Start Smart Sports Development Program, which was unveiled two years later. The program was based on the results of that Northern Kentucky University study, which found that 49 percent of children ages five to ten lack the minimum skills needed to successfully participate in sports. So our goal was to create a sort of "training wheels" program for children.

So what exactly is Start Smart? The staple of the program is a series of specially designed drills that are aimed at improving the basic skills needed for sports, such as throwing, fielding, and hitting in baseball, kicking and catching in football, and dribbling and heading in soccer. The exercises use equipment made of softer, safer materials, all developed by professional physical educators. At the cost of about thirty dollars, parents can give their children such things as a soft, larger-than-normal bat that is easier to hit with; or a glove that would fit any child's hand; or a soft, light, colorful soccer-like ball that kids could kick and experience immediate success with. The entire experience enhances learning, while keeping fun as the top priority. Working one-on-one with their children while rotating through the six different "skill stations," parents have the opportunity to play a significant role in improving their child's proficiency, accuracy, and confidence. The stations are altered during each week of the six-week program to account for the child's overall success.

The real key to Start Smart is that it prepares *the parents* for organized sports. Through the program's special training video, parents are able to see the important role they must play in keeping sports in the proper perspective. While the children are learning the basic skills of sports, the parents, by viewing the video, are developing an understanding of the dangers that lurk if they demand constant excellence or demean their children for a poor performance. This is a key element that has been missing from organized sports in the past. If we can develop positive attitudes and actions in parents and let them know what is expected when their children are this small, then we have nipped a lot of problems in the bud.

"Parents know it's a safe program, and the type of equipment that's used is perfect for this age—especially in terms of color and safety—and that's a big draw for the kids," said Joni O'Toole, program coordinator for the Glastonbury (Connecticut) Parks and Recreation Department. "It's a wonderful opportunity for parents and children to work together on sports skills in a structured setting that's non-competitive and non-threatening."

What have been the results in the communities where Start Smart has been adopted? The outcomes have been very positive, and in a number of different ways. Let me explain.

You may recall the NKU study found that children who enter youth sports programs with fundamental motor skill competence have added confidence in their ability to perform, and are much more likely to improve their skill performance and be successful in competition. These same children are also more likely to continue to participate in physical activities throughout their adult lives.

So one result of the Start Smart program is that the youngsters develop their motor skills, and when the organized program starts, they are ready. "Children who don't have the motor skills are afraid to participate and afraid to fail. But this program says to them, 'Yeah, I can hit, I can throw, I can catch,' so when they do go into organized sports they're doing the same things that they learned in the Start Smart program," said Buddy Collins of North Carolina, who participated with his 4-year-old son.

Recreation directors report that motor skills aren't the only things being learned by the young participants. The children improve their listening skills, follow directions better, and get the chance to interact with their peers, all valuable skills that will be useful not just in sports but as they enter their first years of school.

From a recreation director's point of view, there's another subtle benefit of Start Smart. Because adults also learn how to properly teach sports skills to children, this makes them strong candidates to fill future volunteer coaching spots, a tremendous asset for parks and recreation department leaders, who are always searching for quality volunteer coaches.

Because the initial Start Smart Football program has been embraced by recreation professionals as well as parents, we've taken the program a step further and introduced "Start Smart Baseball" and "Start Smart Soccer." They're designed to introduce children to all the skills necessary for a fun and rewarding experience in those specific sports.

The first "training wheels" for sports are now available, and they have proven to be quite effective. Children and parents nationwide can attest to that.

CONCLUSION

I believe we've reached an important juncture in youth sports. We can make a tremendous difference in the lives of youngsters and put the fun back into their games. We can help children learn life skills better through sports than almost any other medium. We truly have the opportunity in the future to make Johnny—and Mary— not hate sports, but rather to learn to enjoy every wonderful aspect that sports has to offer.

The ideas and programs offered in the preceding pages are just a small sampling of what can be done to insure that all children have a sports participation experience that is positive, memorable, and rewarding. There certainly are many more solutions that you, other parents, coaches, and administrators can come up with on your own to create an environment for children that eliminates or reduces the negative behaviors we have explored and, instead, restores the game to the children.

To paraphrase Senator Edward Kennedy, Some see the future the way it will be and say, "Why?" and others see the future the way it *should* be and say, "Why not?" I urge you to choose your vision of the future of youth sports for your children and ask, "Why not?" Then work with the others in your community to make that vision a reality. To paraphrase our Alliance motto, we *can* make better sports for kids . . . better kids for life.

Conclusion

L et me make it perfectly clear that not every child who participates in organized sports has a bad experience. The problem is that too often the only reason a child has a positive experience is simple good luck. She or he just happened to be fortunate enough to be in the right place at the right time and played for a coach who cared more about the well-being of children than about championships. Or perhaps, the program administrator never wavered from fun and safety. Or maybe the parents involved had a firm grasp of what youth sports are really all about. Unfortunately, today, these are largely the exceptions.

The lack of appropriate philosophy on our playing fields, as well as all the other negative factors we've covered throughout this book, makes it very clear that we need to change the system. The present situation in place nationwide actually facilitates the emotional and physical abuse of children and encourages inappropriate behaviors. The message is clear: Organized sports needs much more than a minor tune-up; it needs a complete overhaul. Making sure Johnny hates sports is certainly not the stated mission of our youth athletics programs. Too often, however, that is the effect.

The organization that I founded back in the 1980s was set up to add a little sanity to the mix. By certifying coaches,

training administrators, orienting parents, accrediting officials, and offering children a safe, fun-filled environment, we
hoped to begin to deal with the host of problems that beset
youth sports. People thought my idea was definitely bizarre
at the time. They felt that, *in principle,* it might be a good idea,
but the thought of youth league coaches, administrators, and
officials going through training programs was a bit off the
wall. Those early rollercoaster years were difficult—emotionally, professionally, and financially. However, with the support of countless people just like you who have picked up
this book, I now find myself with an organization that has
exploded on the youth sports scene, making a tremendous
difference in small towns and big cities across the country.
NYSCA, NYSOA, and all the Alliance organizations are now
a force for good across the nation.

We have arrived, and just in time.

It seems we now have a choice of two roads to follow.

We can continue down one highway to provide programs
that emphasize winning over fun; reward scoreboard-mental-
ity coaches who preach that winning is everything; instill
negative values in young athletes; place untrained and
unqualified individuals in key decision-making roles; feature
out-of-control fans and post-game fisticuffs; belittle safety
issues; and ultimately cause tremendous emotional, psychological, and physical harm to children. We can continue to
take as our models the likes of Vince Lombardi, Bobby
Knight, and the sports professionals. We can continue to suffer all the ills outlined in the early chapters of this book.

Or we can take a different road. We can make a stand, and
exercise leadership for positive change at the local level.

Some people might think this is the more difficult road,
but I think not. Making changes in our current system may
not be as hard as some think exactly *because the resources and
the training programs now exist to restructure our youth programs
with the best interests of the children as their primary objective.*

If we adopt the suggestions offered in this book, we will
promote sports programs for our young people that promote

play rather than strictly competition; introduce a mandatory orientation program for parents; and provide a program to certify the coaches who work with children. We will require community sports teams and leagues to implement national standards before securing playing permits for the use of community and school fields, and require our league administrators to be trained in their responsibilities. We will include handicapped children in our programs and end gender discrimination. We will make safety equipment and safety rules major priorities; insure a code of ethics for parents, coaches, officials, and administrators; and provide training and certification for its officials in all sports. We will provide our youngest players with a preparatory program so they will actually be ready for organized sports when they start.

And we will take as our models, Bill Hughes, who adopted the "Everybody plays" philosophy; Grantland Rice, who wrote, "It's not that you won or lost; but how you played the game"; and Baron de Coubertin, who said, "The important thing in life is not to triumph but to have fought well."

One thing I have learned over the years is that change is not always easy. In fact, most people resent it. But without making the changes I have outlined, we are guilty of doing a tremendous disservice to millions of children. We're taking experiences that should be truly joyous times in so many young lives and turning them into miserable memories filled with heartache and disappointment.

So, the bottom line is this: We must change the face of youth sports in America. If the next generation is to have all the positive experiences and happy memories organized sports can offer, we can't assume that these things will happen all by themselves. As parents, you and I have the strongest motivation to introduce positive change because we want to keep a smile on the face and a bounce in the step of the next generation. Keep that in mind when you stand up at the next meeting of the local league and begin to speak.

In 1981, my family and I took the step to make a difference and risked everything to make our vision come true.

Now, I challenge you to put down this book and join me in doing something in your community. The choice is in your hands. You have the opportunity and the ability to put the fun back into sports, not only for your children, but for their friends and countless other youngsters.

A positive youth sports program should not be something we all just *hope* turns out well in the end. It requires action at the local level. But now we have a plan for action; we have a vision for the future.

Perhaps, today, Johnny, Mary, and many of their friends do hate sports. But, with your help, sports can become not just a source of joy, but also a wonderful learning experience for generations of Johnny's and Mary's to come.

To Get Involved

If you have read this book and are now moved to action, or if you would like further information about any program, product, or organization discussed in the text, please send a 9x12 self-addressed envelope with 99 cents postage to:

National Alliance For Youth Sports
Department WJ
2050 Vista Parkway
West Palm Beach, FL 33411

Or visit the Alliance website on the Internet at:

www.nays.org

About the Author

Fred Engh was born in Johnstown, Pennsylvania, and was raised in Ocean City, Maryland, where he attended elementary and junior high school. He received his high school diploma from Mercersburg Academy in Pennsylvania, where he was a four-year member of the varsity wrestling team. In his senior year, he captained the team and placed second in the National Prep School Wrestling Championships.

After turning down several wrestling scholarship offers, Fred entered the United States Army. After serving two years, he enrolled at the University Maryland, where he was a member of the wrestling team. After his sophomore year, he transferred to the University of Maryland Eastern Shore, where he competed on the golf team. He graduated from the University of Maryland with a Bachelor of Science degree in physical education.

Fred taught elementary education for three years before accepting the head football coaching and athletic director position at St. Elizabeth High School in Wilmington, Delaware in 1966. While coaching, he was also the color commentator for radio station WDEL's football game of the week.

In 1968, Fred gained his first professional experience in the world of organized youth sports when he accepted the position of director of the Catholic Youth Organization (CYO) for Delaware. As director of the CYO, he was responsible for administering programs for over 4,000 participants in football, basketball, baseball, and other sports. He was appointed to the National CYO Athletic Committee in 1970, and was named chairman of the nation's first certification program for coaches.

In 1973, Fred was offered the position of national director of youth sports by the Athletic Institute in Chicago. Created by the Sporting Goods Manufacturers Association to promote sports and physical education throughout the nation, the Institute gave Fred a new means of working towards the improvement of youth sports.

One of Fred's most notable achievements at the Institute was bringing together the leading youth sports organizations in America for the purpose of sharing important information on youth sports administration, coaches' education, parental problems, and other key issues facing youth athletics. It was this initial meeting that led to the development of The National Council of Youth Sports.

In 1977, while still at the Institute, Fred was promoted to executive director of the American Sports Education Institute. He remained in this position until 1980, when he left to lay the groundwork for the creation of the National Youth Sports Coaches Association (NYSCA). As the nation's first membership organization for volunteer coaches in children's sports, this group would turn out to be a significant force in the history of youth athletics. One of its many contributions was the development of a training system designed to educate and hold accountable coaches of youth sports.

By 1993, Fred's program to reform organized youth sports had evolved into the National Alliance for Youth Sports, a nonprofit organization that works to provide safe and fun sports for America's youth. As the founder and president of the Alliance, Fred has been a featured speaker in more than 200 cities throughout America, Europe, and the Far East. He has appeared on CNN, *Dateline NBC*, *20/20*, and numerous other television shows, and has spoken on hundreds of radio shows.

During a lifetime of experience, Fred has examined organized sports from every conceivable angle. He has spearheaded efforts that resulted in the development and implementation of a variety of innovative programs, all of which were designed to tackle the many problems plaguing youth sports programs today.

As a former college athlete and the father of seven children, Fred is a firm believer in the power of positive sports experiences to enhance the all-around development of youngsters. He has devoted his life to making organized sports an enjoyable and rewarding experience for every child.

Fred Engh resides in West Palm Beach, Florida, with his wife, Michaele.

Fred Engh (center) and wife, Michaele,
surrounded by their children and grandchildren.

Index

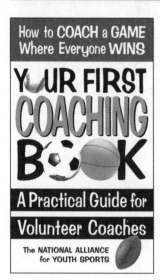

YOUR FIRST COACHING BOOK

A Practical Guide for Volunteer Coaches

by the National Alliance for Youth Sports

For the millions of children involved in youth sports, it is their coach who plays a major role in the way they will feel about playing. It is the coach who is entrusted with the tasks of organizing the team, setting up training activities, managing the game, handling medical crises, and buying pizzas. Unfortunately, few youth sports organizations provide any real training for their coaches. Instead, the volunteers who become coaches must pick up the information on their own or learn as they go. The result for too many children can be seen in the increasingly large percentage of kids who drop out of organized leagues.

To help coaches understand their important role as well as the challenges that lie ahead of them, the National Alliance for Youth Sports—America's premier youth sports advocacy group—has created a simple and straight-forward guide for coaches. In this guide, the coach will learn what factors makes up good coaching, what tasks the coach is responsible for, and how a coach can best deal with the most common problems faced both on the playing field and off. Solidly based on NAYS's twenty-fives years of experience working with youth organizations and children, *Your First Coaching Book* offers sound and practical advice on all key issues.

The National Alliance for Youth Sports is America's leading advocate for positive and safe sports for children. The Alliance features a wide range of programs that educate volunteer coaches, parents, youth sport program administrators, and officials about their roles and responsibilities in the context of youth sports, in addition to offering youth development programs for children. The Alliance's programs are provided at the local level through dynamic partnerships with more than 2,400 community-based organizations, such as parks and recreation departments, Boys and Girls Clubs, Police Athletic Leagues, YMCA/YWCAs, and other independent youth service groups throughout the country and military installations worldwide.

$3.95 • 64 pages • 4 x 7-inch paperback • 2-Color • Sports & Recreation/Reference/Coaching • ISBN 0-7570-0200-5

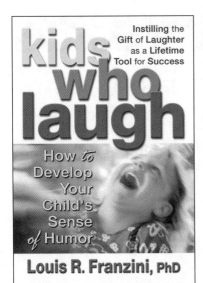

KIDS WHO LAUGH

How to Develop Your Child's Sense of Humor

Louis R. Franzini, PhD

Some are born with a sense of humor—most children are not. As children grow, their use of humor is acquired through various experiences. Unfortunately, most parents never really focus on this important characteristic and have no idea how to instill this learned behavior. *Kids Who Laugh* is the first book to examine the psychology of humor in children and explore the many benefits humor has to offer, including self-confidence, coping skills, self-control, and so much more.

Most important, *Kids Who Laugh* presents the actual tools that parents can use to develop a healthy sense of humor. The author provides a wide array of easy-to-do and fun exercises designed for parents to use with their children, as well as simple strategies that parents can apply to create a customized program for their children. Throughout the book, parents will find practical suggestions, ideas, and advice on incorporating humor into their child's life—as well as a host of resources that can help them do so. Whether it's dealing with teasers or simply making new friends, laughter can make an important difference. With *Kids Who Laugh,* you can give your child a very special present that will last a lifetime—the gift of laughter.

Dr. Louis R. Franzini received his PhD in clinical psychology from the University of Pittsburgh. He is a professor of psychology at San Diego State University in California, where he has taught for over twenty-five years. For over ten years, he has focused his attention on humor research. Dr. Franzini has carefully observed stand-up comedians, has been a stand-up comedian, and has served as president of Laughmasters and Toastmasters International Club. He is the author of two books and numerous articles, and has appeared on radio and television shows throughout North America.

$14.95 • 192 pages • 6 x 9-inch paperback • Parenting / Psychology • ISBN 0-7570-0008-8